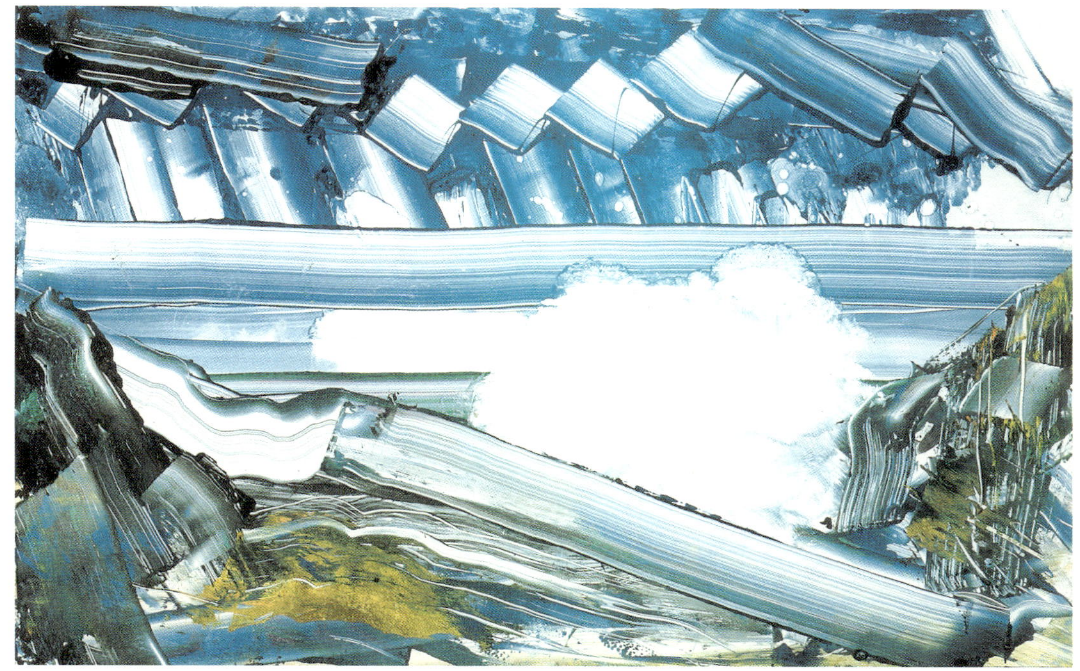

Robert Zandvliet

The Varick Series

Monotypes

Essay by Vincent Katz

Poems by Elaine Equi and Vincent Katz

Peter Blum Edition New York
MM

In the fall of 1999, about a year after my first meeting with Robert Zandvliet, I invited the artist to come to New York to realize a series of monotypes. New York had a powerful attraction for him, a place where one of his predecessors, for whom he had a strong affinity, set foot some 75 years before – a stowaway on the *SS Shelley* – Willem de Kooning.

Robert Zandvliet was prepared for this adventure. The previous spring, on his first visit to New York, I had introduced him to master printer Maurice Sanchez. The size of the monotypes and some ideas for imagery had been carefully worked out beforehand. But it was the capacity to adapt and improvise that eventually became crucial to the successful outcome of this project.

Zandvliet stayed in New York for three weeks, working continuously with tireless energy, interrupted only by nighttime and a short excursion to Long Island. The nights brought forth an ever-growing harvest moon that found its way into several of the monotypes. Likewise, a short but intense visit to De Kooning's landscape around East Hampton seemed to have inspired Zandvliet's imagery.

The proximity to the creative process is one of the great privileges that can accompany the role of the publisher. I want to express my gratitude to Robert Zandvliet for his spontaneity and generosity which allowed me an active role in the creation of *The Varick Series*. To Maurice Sanchez and his associate James Miller my appreciation for their enthusiasm and input in achieving this extraordinary undertaking. My thanks also to Vincent Katz, who not only shared his keen first hand observations in his essay, but together with Elaine Equi, made this publication into a poet / artist dialogue, giving a unique and astonishing dimension to the work of Robert Zandvliet.

Peter Blum
New York, February 2000

A Change In Time:
Robert Zandvliet's Monotypes

by Vincent Katz

I.

In the last years of the 20th century, there was supposedly a resurgence of fascination with painting, against the prevalent backdrop of media-related art. However, much of this "new painting" is really only conceptual art in painting's clothing. It has everything to do with idea—usually in imagery of a provocative sexual or socially "unacceptable" nature—and almost nothing to do with painting. Painting, the art of painting, what we may presume to call real painting, has to do with consummate skill, mastery of techniques, accrued over years of nose-to-the-grindstone effort, which enables the artist to create objects of spellbinding and convincing depth and resonance—objects whose impact cannot be replicated (an artwork that is just as good in reproduction is not an interesting artwork). If this reeks of the myth of the artist holed up in his garret, refining his craft, until he is discovered and unleashes his talent and vision on an unsuspecting world, it is because the myth is true, because talent is undeniable. It is the feeling one gets at a concert when the singer sings her first note or the guitarist first strikes his strings—tonight I'm in good hands.

Robert Zandvliet was born in 1970 in Terband, Holland. From 1987 to 1992, he studied at an art school in Kampen, where he was able to do a lot of painting. He did some informal study in Amsterdam from 1992 to 1994, then moved to Rotterdam, where he now lives and works. He likes Rotterdam because, as he says, it's relaxed and working class, which is a casual way of saying that it is far removed from the hype of the familiar art centers. Zandvliet lives in a city, but it is a landscape sparse in contemporary art. He has intentionally separated himself from such issues of the last two decades as person, identity, and appropriation. Rotterdam also happens to be the birthplace of Willem de Kooning.

Although Zandvliet lives in relative artistic isolation, he is part of an important tendency in contemporary art, which is involved with re-examining the tradition of painting and finding new avenues for it. Among the younger artists who have decided to invest in expanding their skill, three in particular, coming from Europe, have affinities—the Londoner Merlin James, Thomas Scheibitz from Germany, and Zandvliet. All three make paintings which are highly proficient, all three make provocative use of color, and all three flit back and forth nervously between abstraction and representation. In terms of color, Scheibitz is the most harsh of the three, experimenting with confectionery tones whose artificiality links them assiduously to the contemporary world. James and Zandvliet, more obviously inspired by earlier artists – more obscure ones in James' case, brighter and more well-known in Zandvliet's – use colors familiar to us from nature and other paintings, though their use of them is native to their own sensibilities.

Scheibitz tends to paint strongly outlined shapes with clear directions. They are not unlike Zandvliet's earliest paintings, which had clearly outlined central images, such as a camera, a movie screen, or a pair of bobby pins. Both artists evinced a fascination with the everyday, albeit more explicitly in the case of Zandvliet. Recently, Zandvliet has moved towards imagery reminiscent of James', that is to say, mysterious scenes with a mythological or fairytale air. Both artists paint, among other things, imagined landscapes – more like innerscapes, in which traditional perspective does not need to hold, natural colors are boldly substituted, scale ruptured, and artifice accentuated. None of these interventions is achieved brusquely. James, in particular, usually works on a small scale, and his paintings are deceptively aggressive. Zandvliet paints big, in bold colors, but with mellifluous technique and color harmonies that mask his subversive intent.

Cecily Brown and John Virtue are two artists close to Zandvliet in terms of the problem of post-abstract-expressionist abstract painting. There is the danger, in reviving any technique or style, of being simply antiquarian. Cecily Brown tries to preclude having her technique simply read as nth generation Ab Ex by submerging specific erotic imagery in it. Zandvliet early on avoided the problem with large, blunt subjects. Lately, he has retreated from that position, emboldened by an interest in landscape, to try to find a halfway point between representation and abstraction. This is similar to what John Virtue does in his recent paintings of the Exe Estuary. In his large painting *Landscape 588,* low-lying land and water are dominated by a melodramatic conflict between brushy black and white forms (drips included). In some of these paintings, Virtue designs scenes carrying across triptych and tetraptych formats. Perhaps he, like Zandvliet in his large tripartite monotypes, wants to impose an element of obvious artificiality to further distance himself from traditional landscape. It is worth noticing, as mentioned above, that none of these artists is American. Perhaps there is more at stake in extending European traditions for artists coming from a European background.

One of Zandvliet's prominent revivals is the totemic, almost hallucinogenic, use of the brushstroke. There are other contemporary artists who use the brushstroke non-ironically, making strokes that stand as centralized images – pure concentration left untouched. Zandvliet differs in introducing the conflict of purity versus difficulty self-imposed. In the current monotype project, he has gone farther than in his paintings towards pure abstraction, while enlarging his range of improvisatory techniques.

II.

Zandvliet: A Log

While Zandvliet was making these monotypes, I visited the print workshop, Derrière L'Etoile, under the direction of Maurice Sanchez, where I was able to see artist and printer at work. Following are some observations, in the form of a diary. In it, I refer to Zandvliet as R.

3d day Thurs Oct 14 1999

"Some things are coming back all the time, like trees." R. looks up with penetrating blue eyes. He is working on his suite of monotypes, almost too fast for the eye to follow his decisions, changes, and marks. "I started out with a lot of grey. I had to get used to the contrast," he says. Some images he does twice, that is to say, he paints the same composition differently. While most are black and white, some are in a chalky green. "On the second day, I became more aware of the white parts." He made some with black images on green backgrounds but was dissatisfied. "It became too separated." A solvent creates "sponging areas," where R. effects washes or tumults of watered-down color that contrast with the dominant, highly present strokes. R. moves towards bold statements, and it is informative to observe how he arrives at them. This is only his third day at work, and he has quickly moved through experimentation to readiness to attack the large-scale monotypes. At first, he did some tests, just as a warm-up, then a series of some 40 medium-sized monotypes all in his first two days. He has, around the studio, many dashed-off pencil sketches on scraps of paper, whose images resemble those he ends up making into monotypes. As with his technique, which he has worked out through constant repetition, he creates images through variations in sketches. When it comes time to begin a monotype, though, he rarely refers to his pencil sketches. With the variations in mind, he jumps into the task of making the monotype, relying on that past experience in imaging.

He is working toward increased scalar complexity, as he gains familiarity with the medium and format. In addition to the difference in size, a significant difference between the medium and large monotypes is that the medium ones are done on a single plate, while the large ones, whether vertical or horizontal, are all triptychs, made by applying pigment over a series of three plates. There were logistic reasons for this choice (Sanchez had recently sold a press which handled larger plates), but also, artist and publisher took the decision to make this extensive body of work with the knowledge that two straight lines would be dividing each large print. R's images are so flowing and circuitous that the persistent rectilinear would seem *a priori* to be a disadvantage, but he works with it, sometimes obscuring the lines in backgrounds composed of similar parallels, other times, more brashly, by echoing the tripartite division the lines engender. His horizontal pieces, in particular, often divide into three sections with tumults of activity on the two sides and relative calm in the middle; or sometimes the reverse strategy. In other pieces, he makes muscular, throbbing shapes that writhe upward at or near the location of the lines.

R's earlier work has much to do with horizontality — both natural and man-made — and in the monotypes, he brings a seasoned arsenal of compositional ploys to the horizontal framework. In his verticals, he seems more often to get stuck in a seemingly prosaic image, which may be an opacity, behind which a subtler future statement is being worked out. He moved quite a way during the making of these monotypes, if one compares them to his previous work, mainly tempera on canvas. It was while making these monotypes that he first made purely abstract images, while simultaneously expanding his technical options. His paintings always derived from a measured, layered approach, while in the monotypes he was able to be much more freewheeling.

In explaining an image, he said he thought of it looking like a *coulisse,* the French word for a flat piece of scenery on the side of a stage. He made a sketch to clarify, and again it was a horizontal image — the stage with flats on the sides, with the added appeal of the frame created by the proscenium.

He uses different spirits — one to clean the plates and another to make the greys. He works rapidly on the plates, often altering marks by erasing the interior of a previously painted stroke, so that it comes out looking ghosted. He likes to obfuscate his skill with certain set tactics, like using ragged pieces of cardboard to guide some of his marks. Then he picks up a rag soaked in the damping spirit and works it into the image. After about 15 minutes, he is getting something he likes, and he slows down. He makes one or two more marks, pulls off his gloves, and tells Maurice it's ready to print. Before you have time to catch your breath, Maurice picks up the left plate and, separating a thin film at the plate's edge, whips the plate from the work table to the press. He aligns the plate on the J.M. Mailänder flatbed press (Stuttgart Bad Cannstatt M 7372), locks it in, and is rolling the huge sheet of paper over it. The image transfers to a drum and from there to the paper. He rolls it back over the paper and back again — three cycles making six passes of ink to paper. He puts the first plate back on the work table, wipes down the drum. He takes the second plate to the press, registering it very carefully, then repeats the rolling process, wipes down the drum a second time, and does it all over for the third and final plate. The prints are printed in a double reverse process, the ink going from the plate to a drum and from there to the paper resulting in an image in the same orientation in which R. composed it, not reversed, as is the case in simple plate-to-paper printing.

After the print has been pulled, R. gets the plates back on the table and immediately wipes black all over them, then starts rubbing some of it off. He moves around to the other side of the table (what was the top from his previous position), begins wiping out a lot of black. Now, back at the original bottom, there is suddenly a long horizontal streak (made by dragging a rag) dipping to the left. He begins working from the top of the image with a brush that looks like a broom, making a dense ground. He then wipes part of it out with a rag. He works swiftly and confidently. People are talking in the background, laughing. The radio plays classical music (WQXR, a Dutch orchestra). He goes back to the bottom and works on the streak area by hand. "This ink is quite sticky," he offers, "I have to use a lot of solvent." This seems more like a captain's assessment of weather conditions than an explanation. With hand-ripped cardboard shapes as guides, he paints diagonal forms with a thick brush he has picked up. This brush's hairs are set in an oval format about seven to eight inches wide and two inches deep. He wipes with a rag along the shapes he's just painted, again using the cardboard to guide himself. He sees forms in his mind's eye and uses the cardboard to limit the brush's path as he follows the form, often elaborating with additional marks. He knows what the cardboard will achieve. He adds marks with a small (three inch) blocky brush and does some strokes with brush alone (no cardboard). His actions become a little less frequent. There is more analysis, more waiting. He clears around the top edge of a curving form, which is the print's central image. His "thoughts" are in place. He looks at Maurice and smiles. "Should we try it?" Again, about 15 minutes have elapsed.

6th day Tues Oct 19 1999

Today there seems to be more contrast—a simultaneous opening of un-inked stretches on certain areas of the plates, combined with denser, thicker blacks than in earlier efforts. R. still moves with determined rapidity, but seems more pre-occupied. A quick hello, a smile, and he stays immersed in the work. More is at stake now, further along. He knows what the medium and format offer, and he knows these are no longer "test runs." These have to be the real thing, one's consummate art, keepers. Glenn Gould's 1981 recording of the Goldberg Variations plays on the radio, appropriately —the sad empathy of eternity's excellence, a cold comfort but there. It seems R. might be finished with this monotype. He looks up, about to say something, moves some bottles and rags out of the way. Then suddenly he loads up his big brush, grabs a long piece of cardboard, and using its straight side, begins making strong, slightly diagonal verticals in the central panel. After a minute or so of this, he changes from brush to rag and continues the same tree-like, leaning shapes. He wipes carefully at one of the un-inked areas, stops to look. Maurice, laughing, calls him to look at something. He goes over politely, oblivious to the joke, and returns immediately to his work. He takes off his gloves and dries his hands at a small fan. Maurice, suddenly serious, examines, then picks up the first plate, begins aligning it on the press.

12th day Weds Oct 27 1999

Today R. is making small plates for the deluxe edition of the book. He finishes off the second as I
walk in. Unlike the medium and large monotypes, these small pieces make ample use of color,
relating them more directly to R.'s previous work in painting. "With these," he explains, "there's more
a feeling of making small paintings, although there are things you could never do in a painting.
When you do a painting, it has to be good the first time. With a plate, you can rub it off again."
Again, there's that sense of a captain guiding himself through uncertain waters. As an explanation,
it doesn't really hold water. First, you *can* rub down a painting, and second, R. hardly ever rubbed
down a plate. He did a lot of rubbing, but not to start all over again; rather, his rubs were part of
his technical language. With these small pieces, R. often works in pairs, using the same image a
second time, with changes. The first pass always looks sharper, brisker; the second more muted.
"In the middle period of the large monotypes, we often did two versions," he adds. In the pair on
which he is currently working, three big trees dominate the scene. The background changes from
plate to plate. R. uses tasteful colors–European in the best sense of the word. They are colors that
remind you of a museum, interior colors, colors of paintings as opposed to natural colors. A bright
yellow, a strong reddish brown. "In painting," he says, "you're more able to separate the colors. In
these monotypes, the colors get blended." They do three passes of two images. With each pass,
certain colors–a blue in this case–become more evident. They emerge from the recesses of the
pigment to be revealed more brightly. The third pass is the most brilliant and blended of all. A
perfect mix, it would seem, but R. decides to do another pass on this third version with a blue
film. Unfortunately, this deadens the image a little and gives an overly greenish cast to the greens
and yellows already present. "Oh well," says R. "We'll have to do another one." It's a little like black-
jack. He is already at work on a new little plate, making squarish scrapes into a deep blue
pigment he has laid down. He trusts the working process, knowing he'll find solace there. Adeptly,
he wipes away, leaving a row of cloud-like shapes. His wipes have the presence of actual brushstrokes. They become invisible strokes, negative strokes, revealed by the artist's alchemical
wizardry against the mass of other marks. He begins working on a second small plate, using ripped
paper edges as guides, small-scale versions of the cardboard ones he used on the large prints. It is
pleasurable watching R. work. His focus has a soothing effect on the viewer, as perhaps it does on
the artist. On the other hand, the printed results are often turbulent, perhaps reflections of the
artist's mental states. There is an inner core of calm, though, to R.'s turbulence. He blots some
over-pigmented sections on the first plate, using a piece of paper with some pencil sketches on it,
fueled by the same resolve with which he does all his work. He then goes over the blotted section,
adding some bright yellow to the otherwise dark area.

In the small color pieces, the relation to nature is more pronounced. The light is more specific (clearer). An arbitrary mark becomes determinate the instant it is laid down. Pulls of parallels' crazy force. Strange photographic-emulsion-like buttons. Twist of a tree-trunk-like form bent by years' growth, wind, environment.

In this 15 day period, R. has completed 48 large monotypes. From those, a certain number will be selected to form the final group. Now we can relax a little. We go out with Peter for a Japanese meal and talk. "I wanted to paint a waterfall," R. says, "but it didn't work out. In a painting, you have to think more clearly. In monotype, you can try it out. When I started painting landscapes, they were quieter. Then I wanted to make them more apocalyptic. Now the monotypes are more complex than the paintings. I want to keep the romantic feel of the paintings but make it more abstract. When you make a big painting, you have to be more aware of what you're doing. You start with lighter colors—yellows—and work to dark. With monotypes, you can clean the Mylar surface and get the white of the paper back." Hearing these words from R., I can only think of how de Kooning's influence still looms so large over all those who would make the active (not ironic) brushstroke part of their vocabulary. I think of de Kooning's obsessive working and re-working of the same canvas. I think of de Kooning's scrapes and negative shapes, his sinuous tubular forms, and how he worked to create material obstacles on which his facility, foundering, could arrive at fresh results—all of which have relevance in regard to R.'s work. I am beginning to see that the difference is that R. does have to be good the first time. He is less concerned with process than was de Kooning. He has committed himself to a range of traditional techniques, but his vision is faster than de Kooning's. He wants to see something, try to capture it, and move on to the next image. That is the connection between his early images of man-made objects and his most abstract work, which appeared in some of the large monotypes.

His horizontal images are more complex than his verticals. Perhaps it is his experience in painting horizontally that has availed him in the monotypes. Certainly, it is a natural propensity of his to view the lay of the land. In the three-part division to the monotypes, he is working with and against the divisions. He is also working with the historical frameworks of religious triptychs and *cadavres exquis.* His composition is of texture as well as image. Each horizontal has a different tone and strategy. In the horizontals, the scale is vast. The verticals are more like scenes from a story. R. plays with the sweeping texture of large brushstrokes, turning graceful parallels into dense fabrics on which the eye can rest. These are not all-over images, despite their activity. The eye is invited to pause on availabilities of light and sound. The continuation of different techniques and shapes adds up to statements like voice-leading in music, one instrument picking up the melody where another has left off.

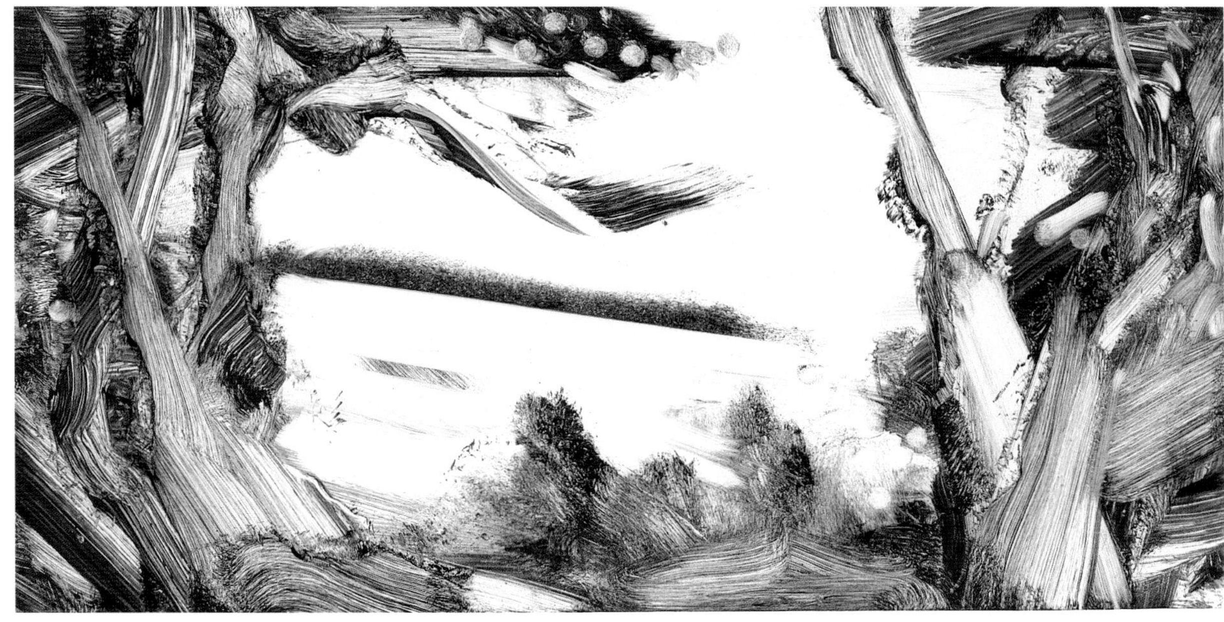

IX, 10. 12. 99

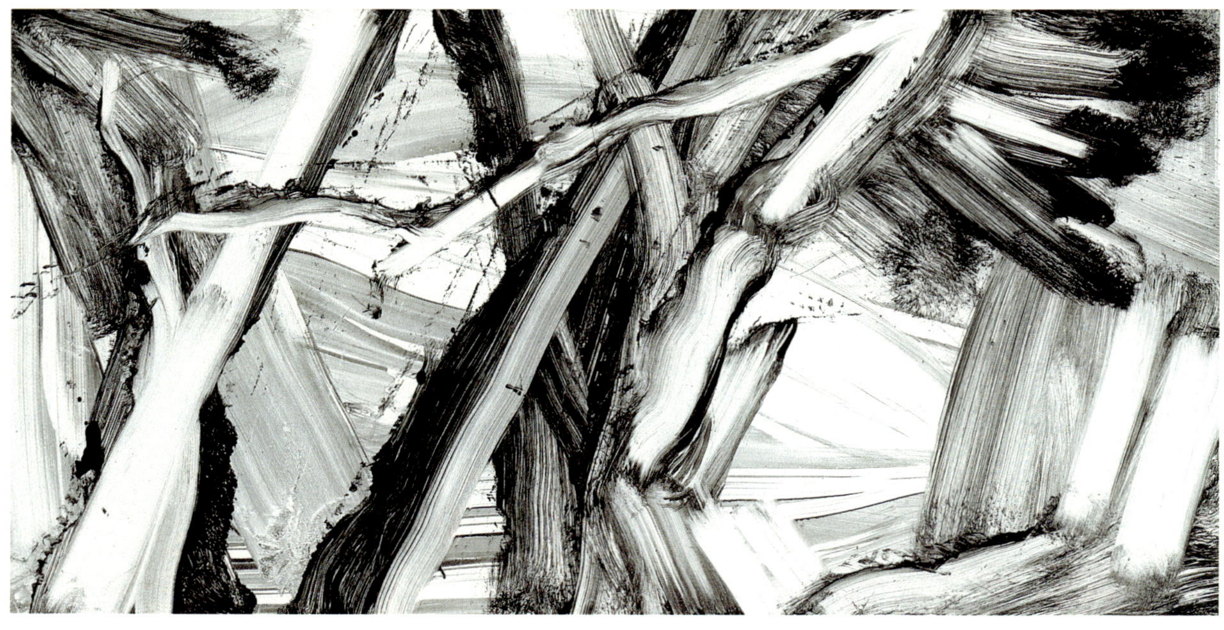

XXI B, 10. 12. 99

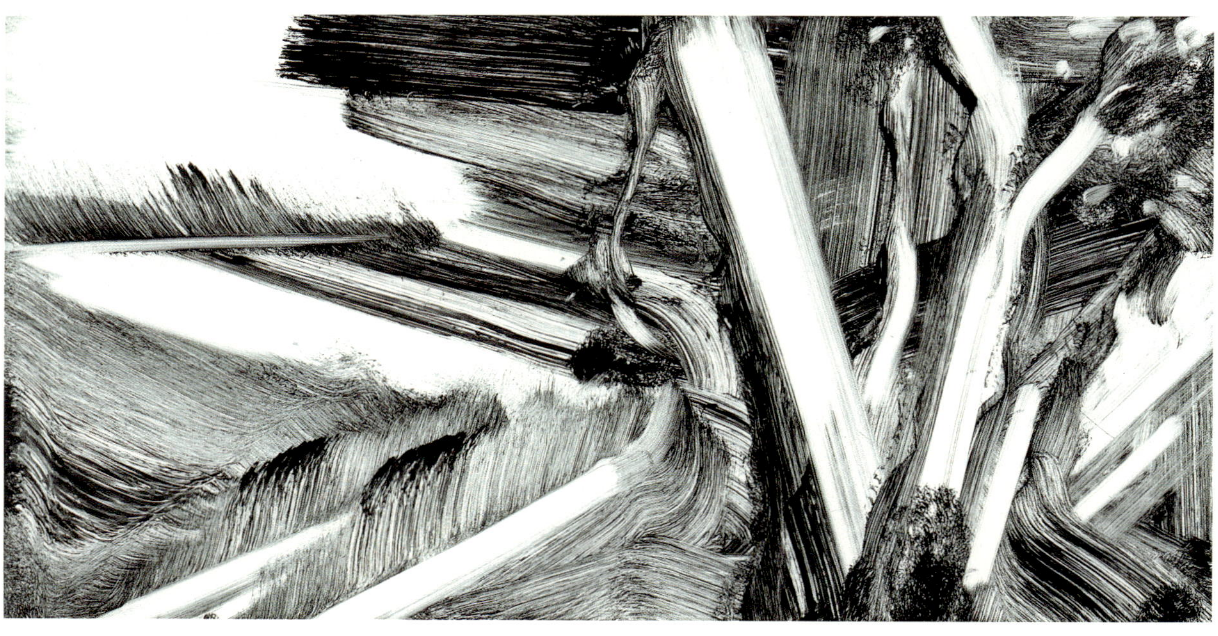

XII, 10. 12. 99

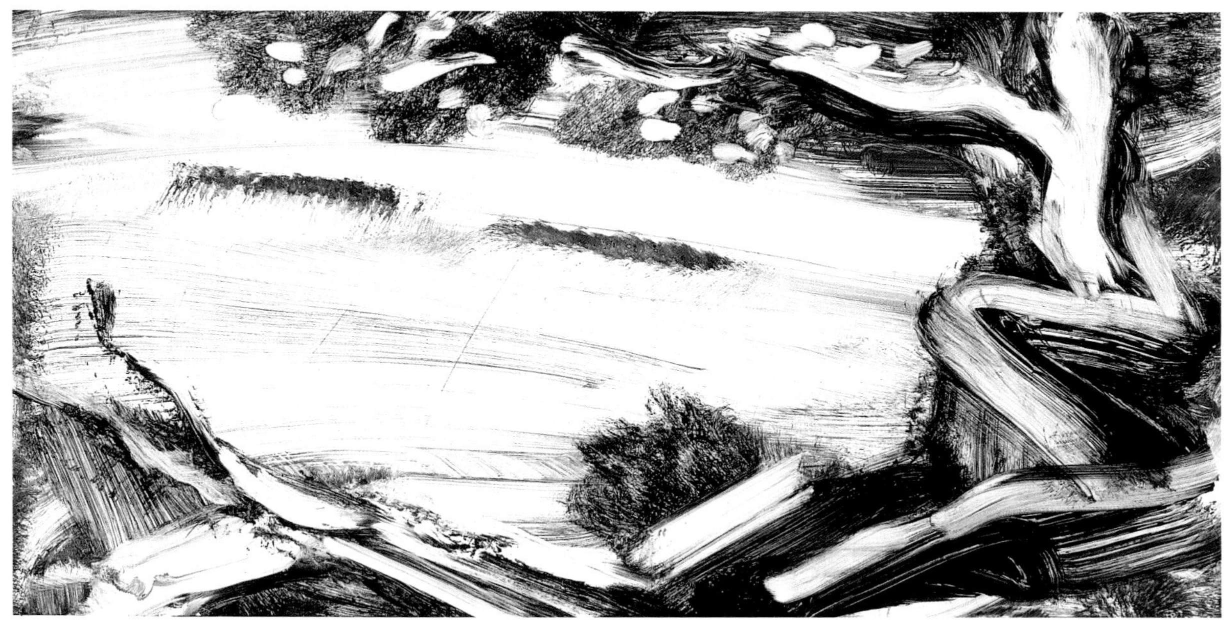

XV, 10. 12. 99

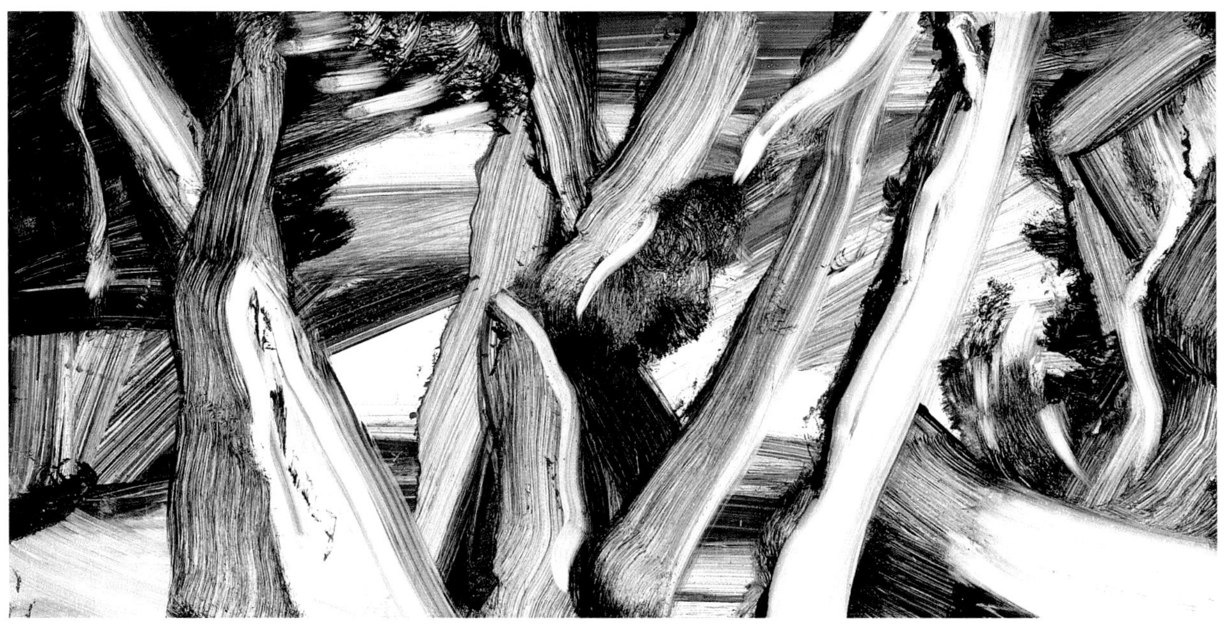

XVII, 10. 12. 99

A poem by

Vincent Katz

Six poems by

Elaine Equi

Opacities

of early morning

pinions thrusting

at odd ends

a sorrowful must

minute's return

to be figured

flung a dense

resource nodded

at prodded

for once a given

solid fold

research wile

beset aloof

kindled in

A Bend In The Light

A bend in the light.

A dross in the drift.

A tilt in the storm.

A gleam in the ditch.

A grace in the gloom.

A kink in the sand.

A spring in the fire.

A lilt in the hand.

A snare in the common.

A hare in the shed.

A mesh in the fury.

A glare in the blurring.

A stretch in the arc.

A pulse in the bark.

A fork in the wave.

A heft in the sway.

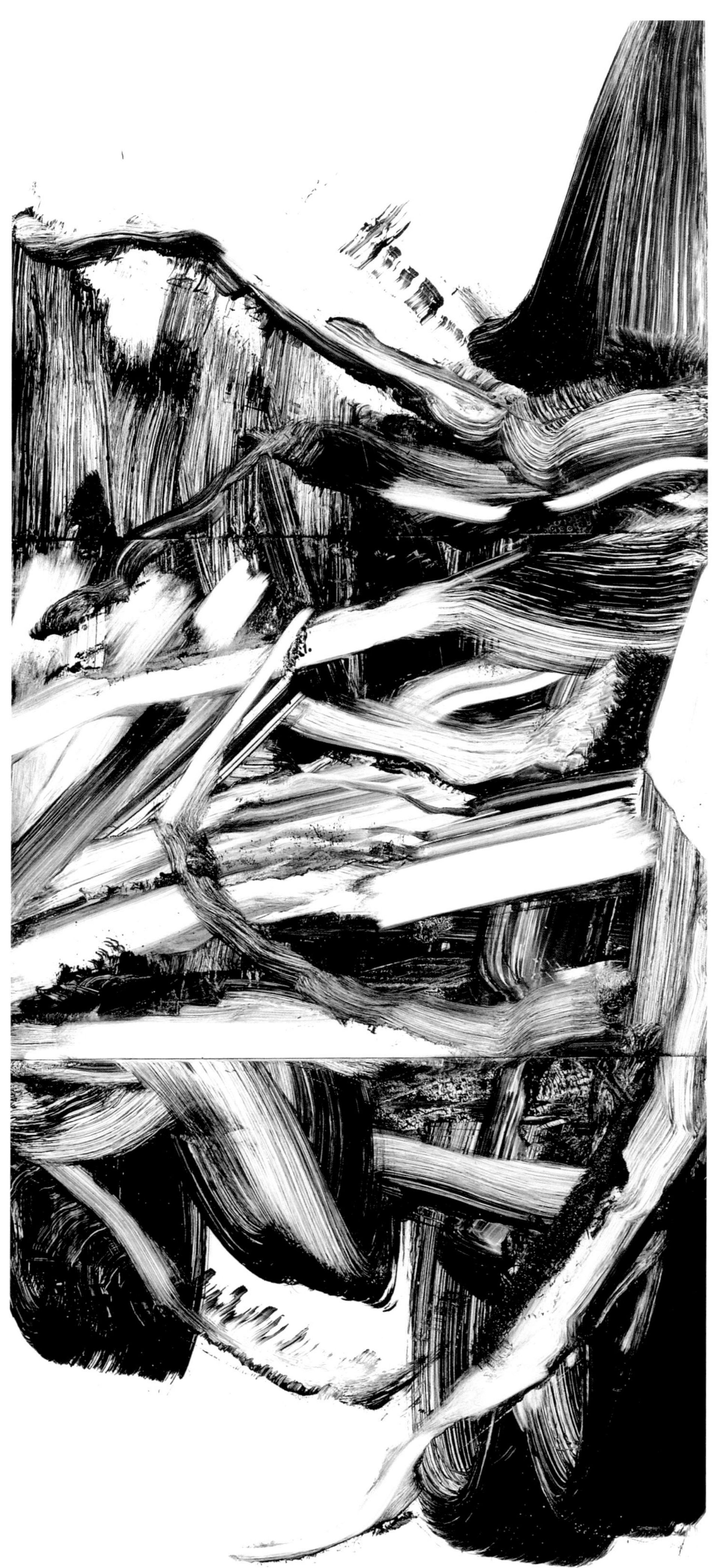

II, 10. 14. 99

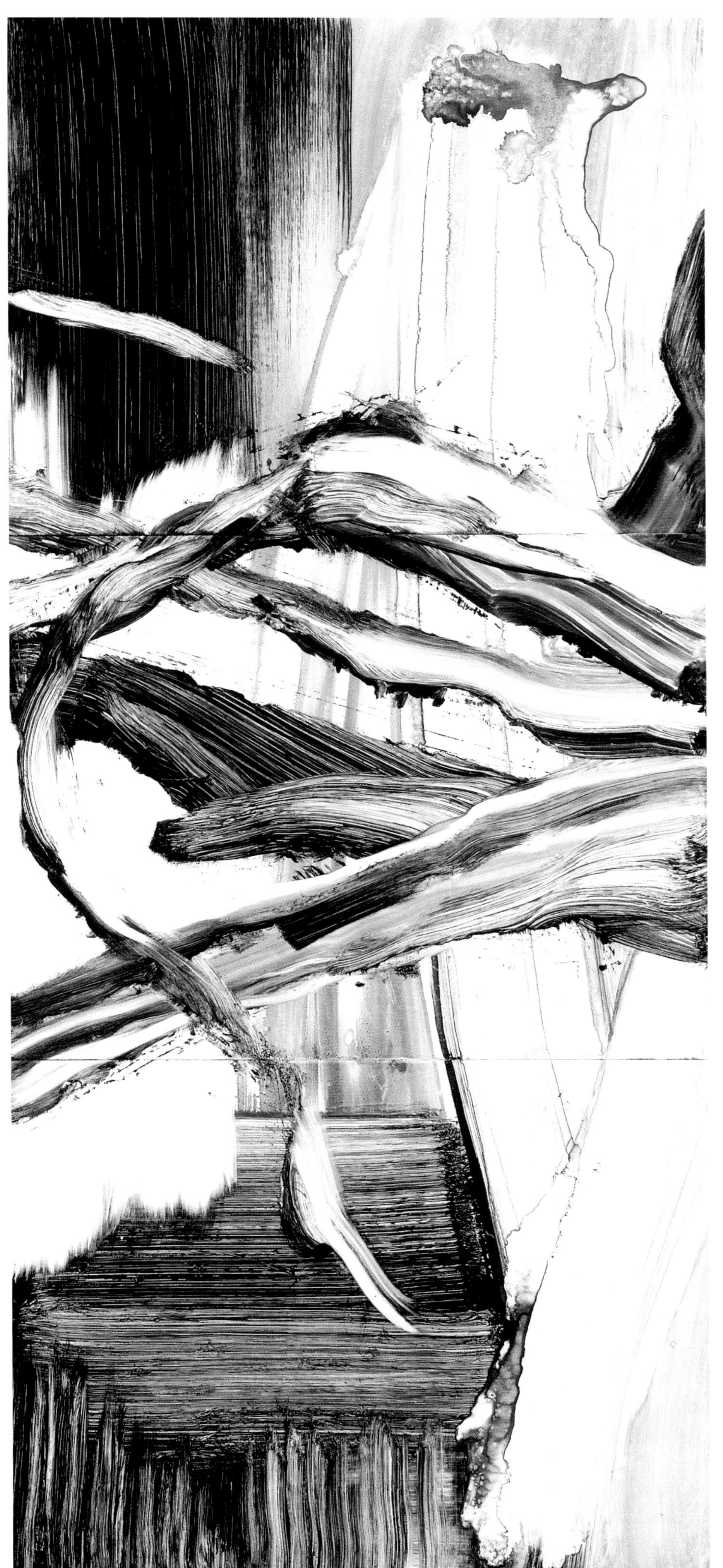

III B, 10. 14. 99

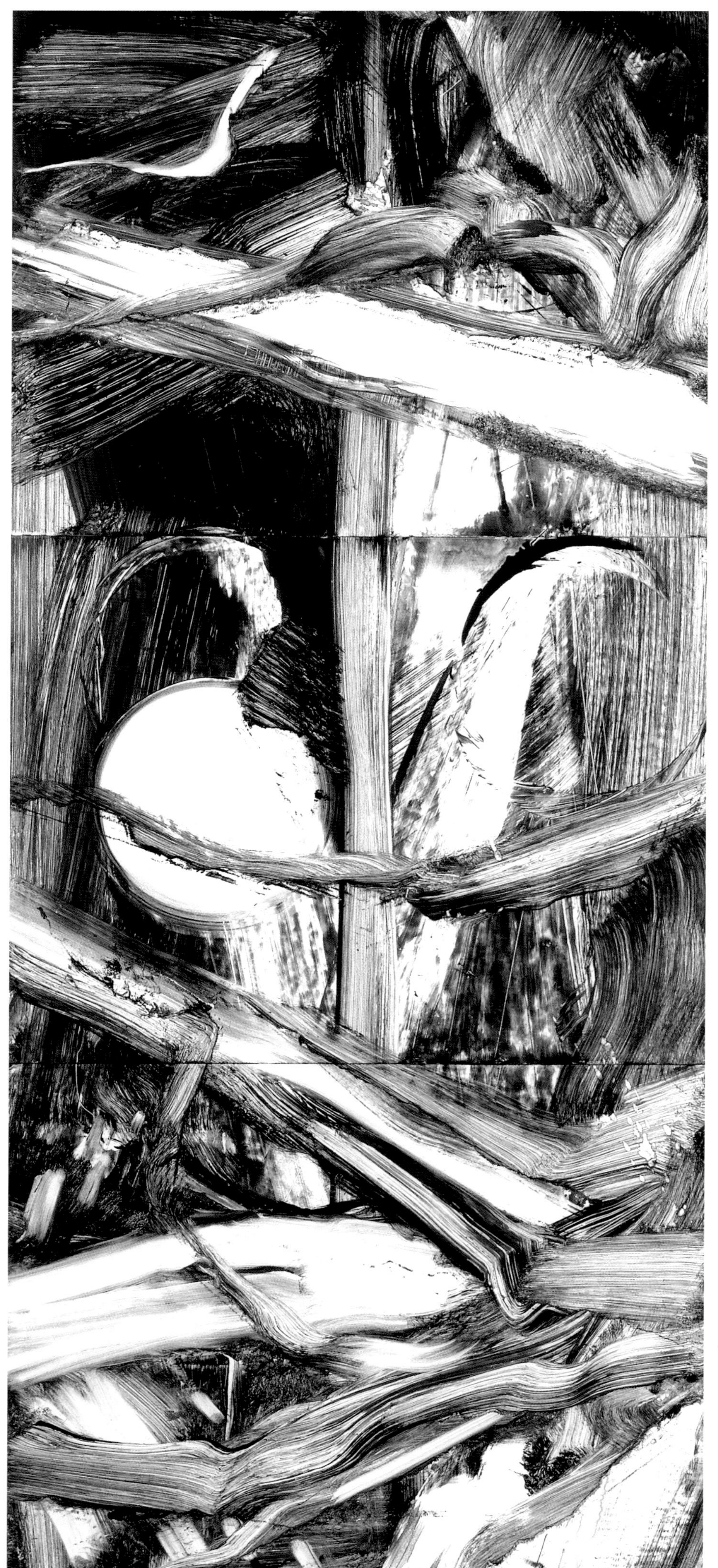

IV, 10. 14. 99

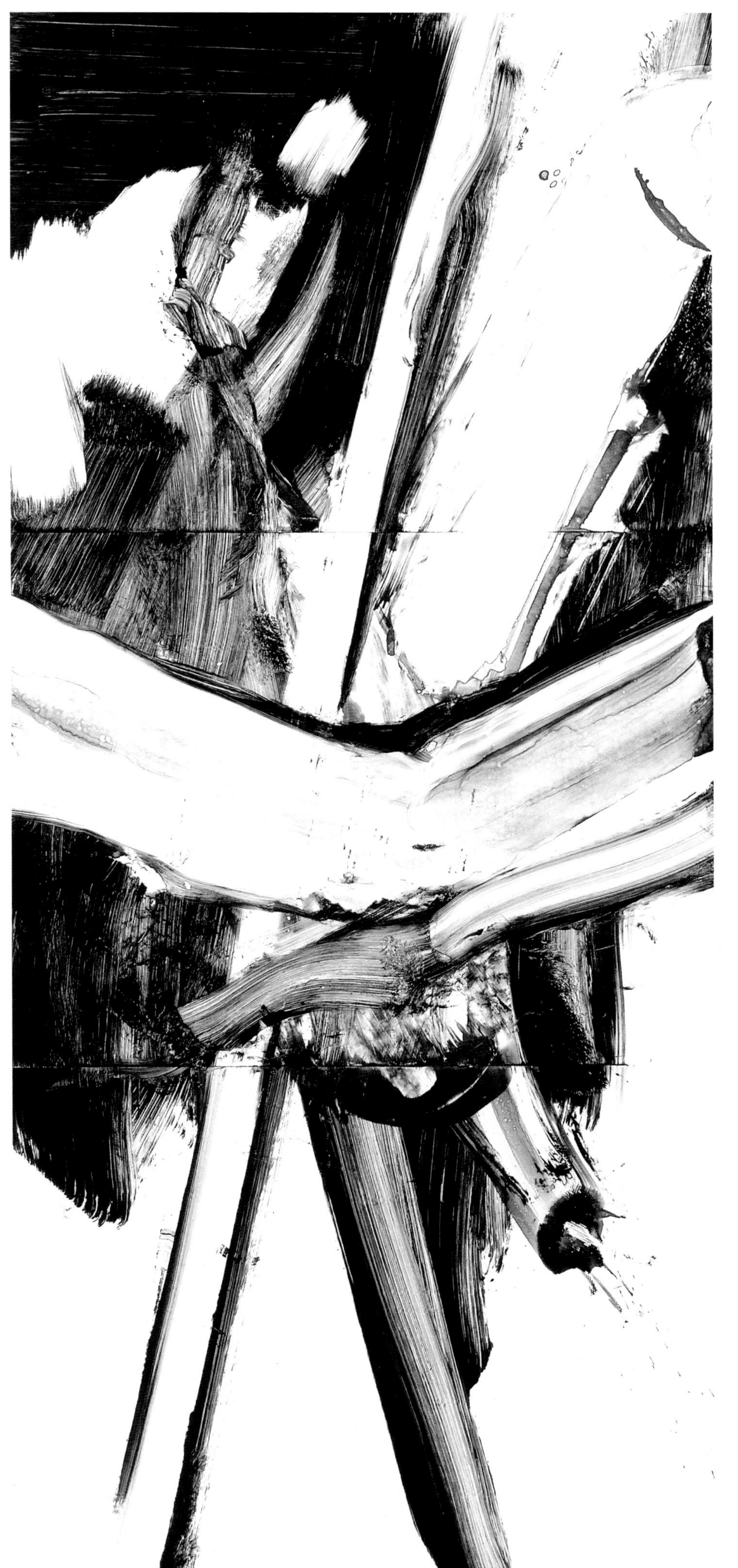

V, 10.14.99

astride the

Jolly Roger

roads' inway

collapseable

snow insert

breast feeling

crested align

jib up saloon

rim of sky

pack oak

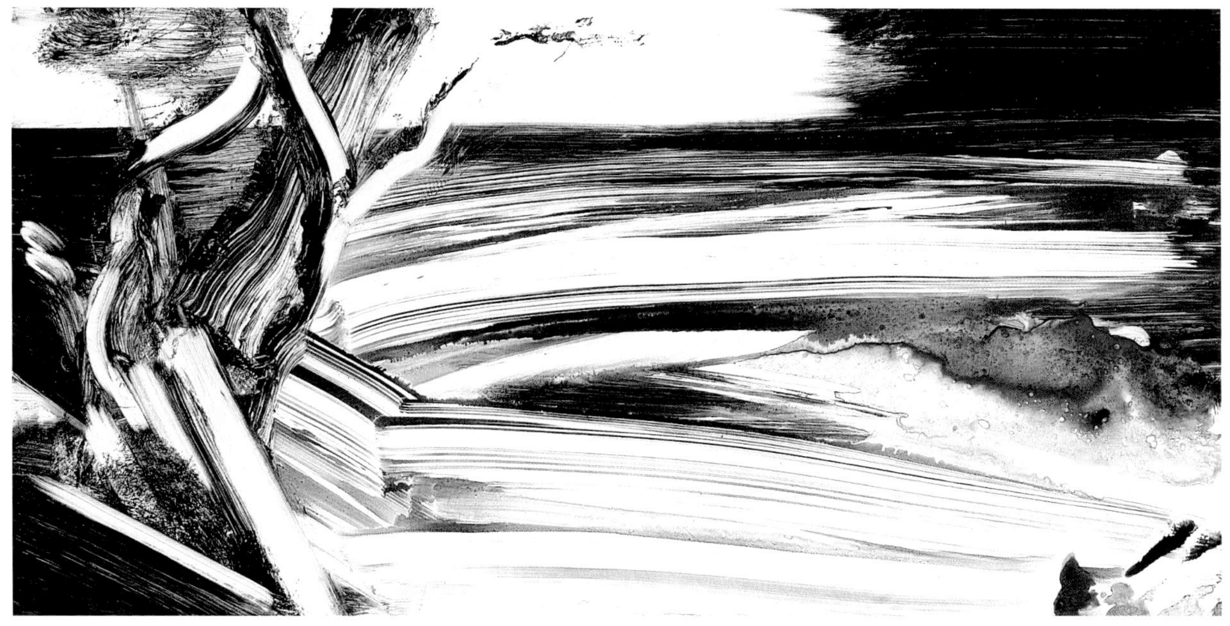

XX, 10. 13. 99

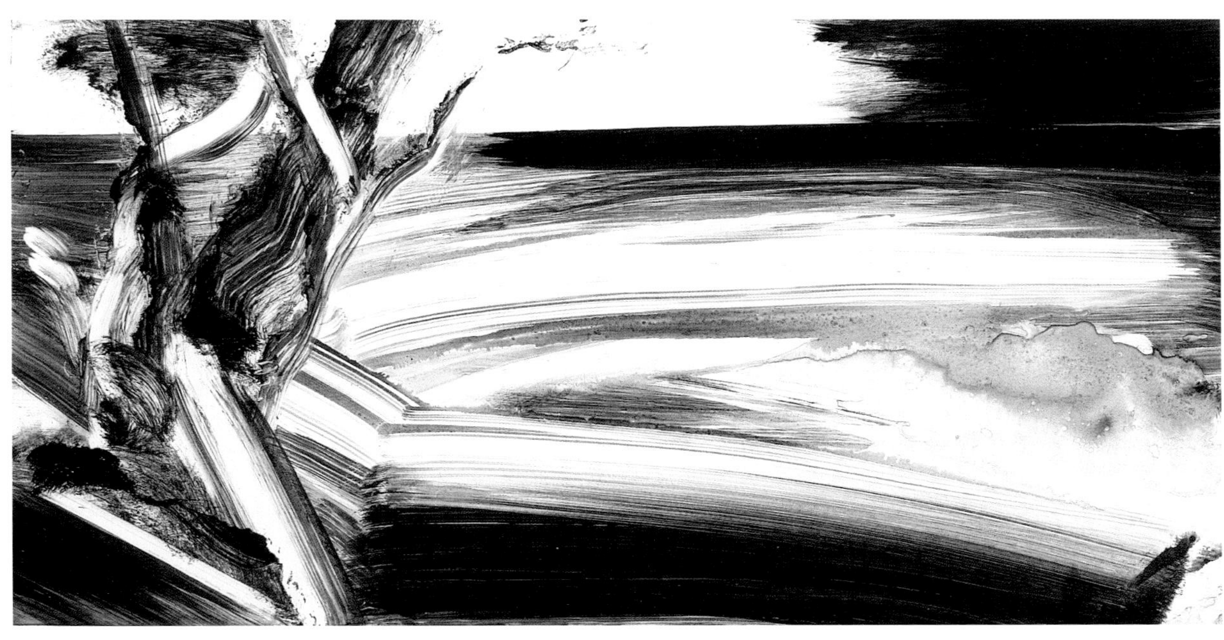

XXI A, 10. 13. 99

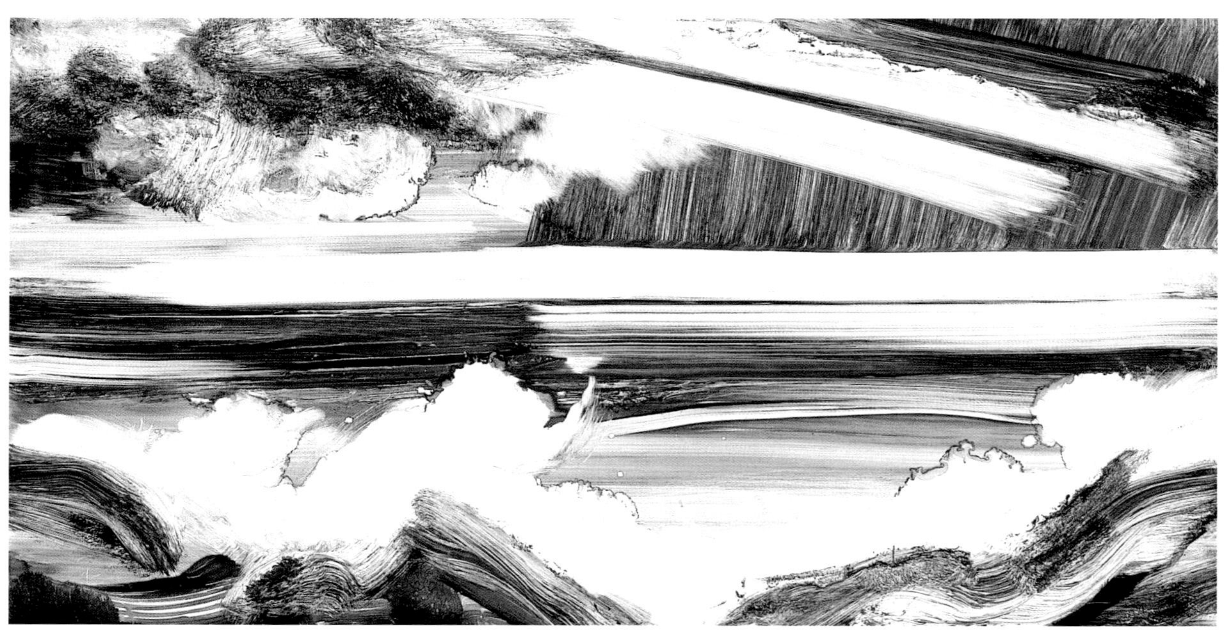

XI A, 10. 13. 99

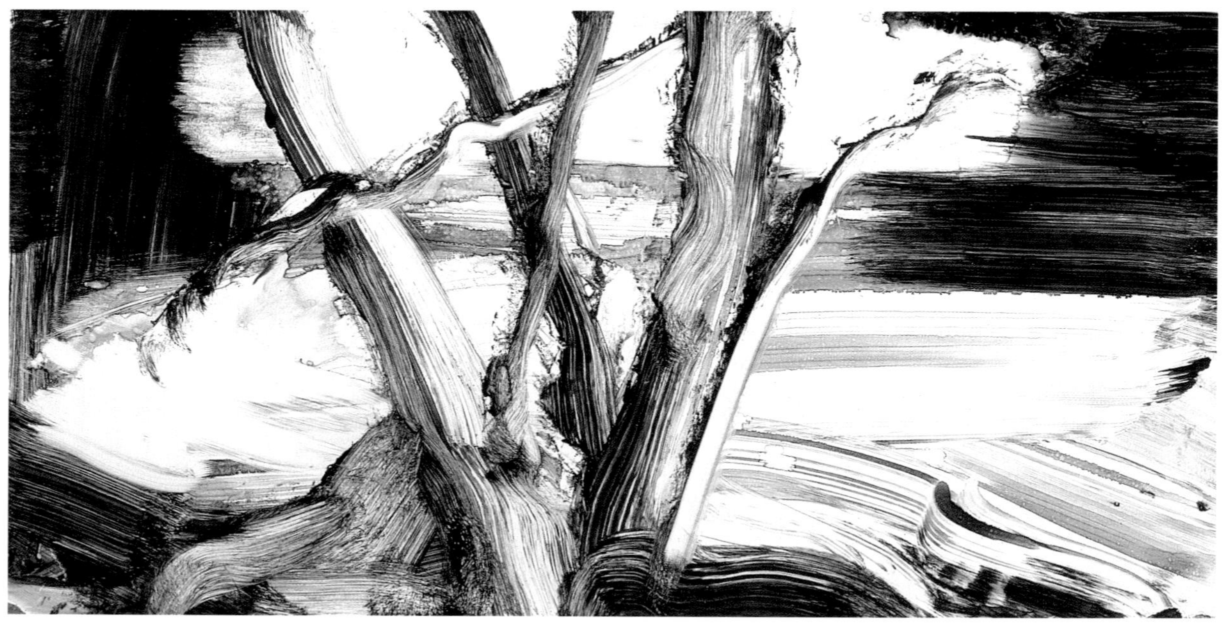

XXII, 10. 13. 99

Fogetting

backwards.

    For getting behind.

    For getting around.

    For getting down

flat as the land.

One sees nothing but light

climbing back

    leaf by leaf

clinging, clanging.

Drinking all day

    through a green tube.

Surge. Halt.

Halt. Surge. Surge.

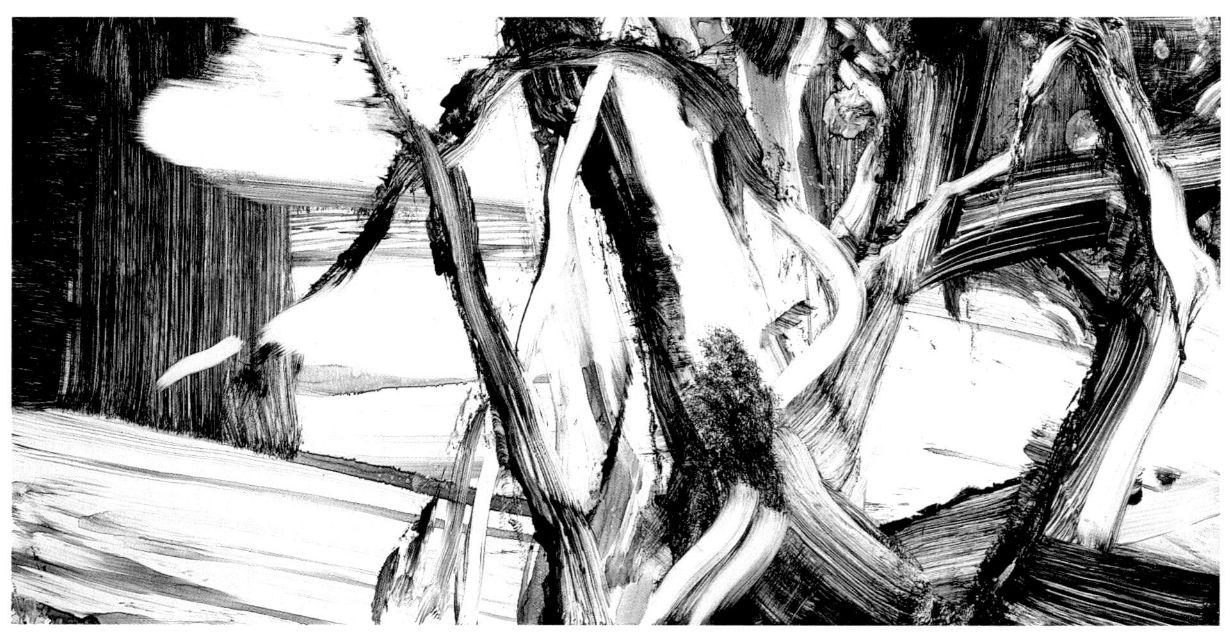

XXIII, 10. 13. 99

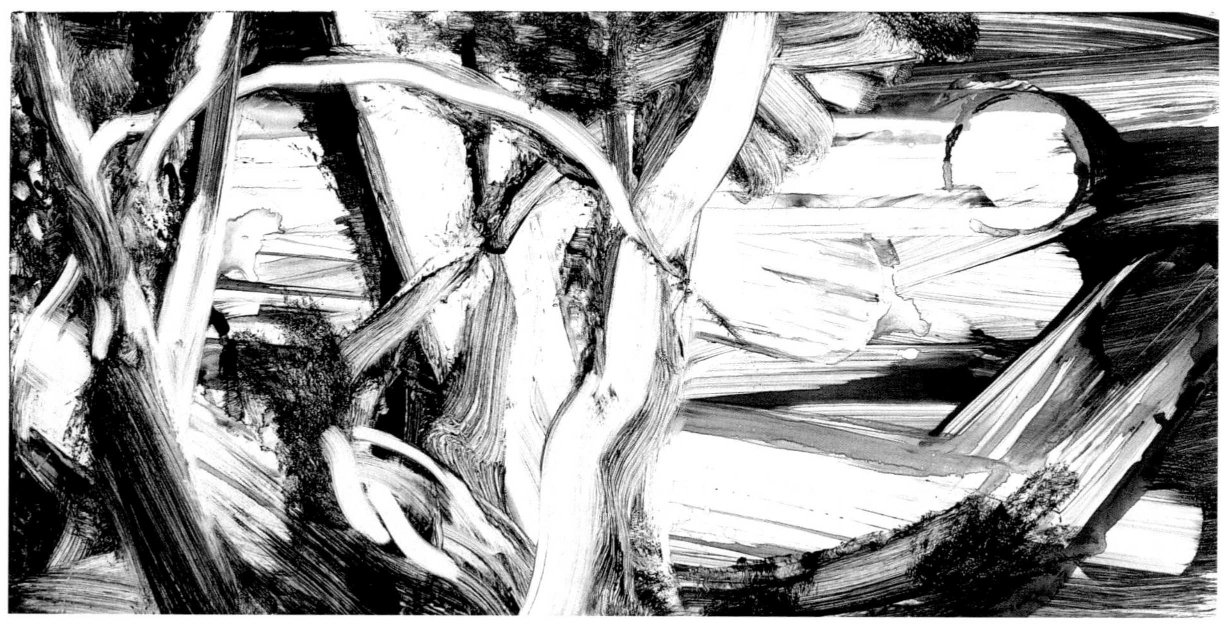

XXIV, 10. 13. 99

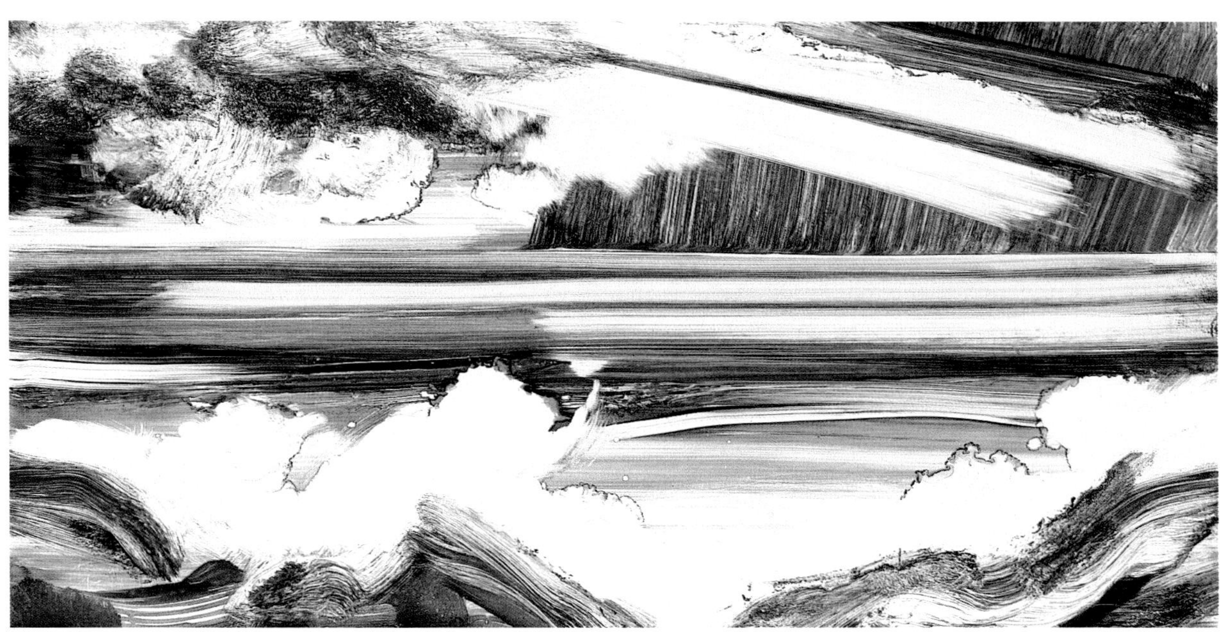

XXV, 10. 13. 99

norwesting

assails

senses

adrift

pinned on

nervous hoax

deprived

no guarantee

icy humps

siphon

into

pocket

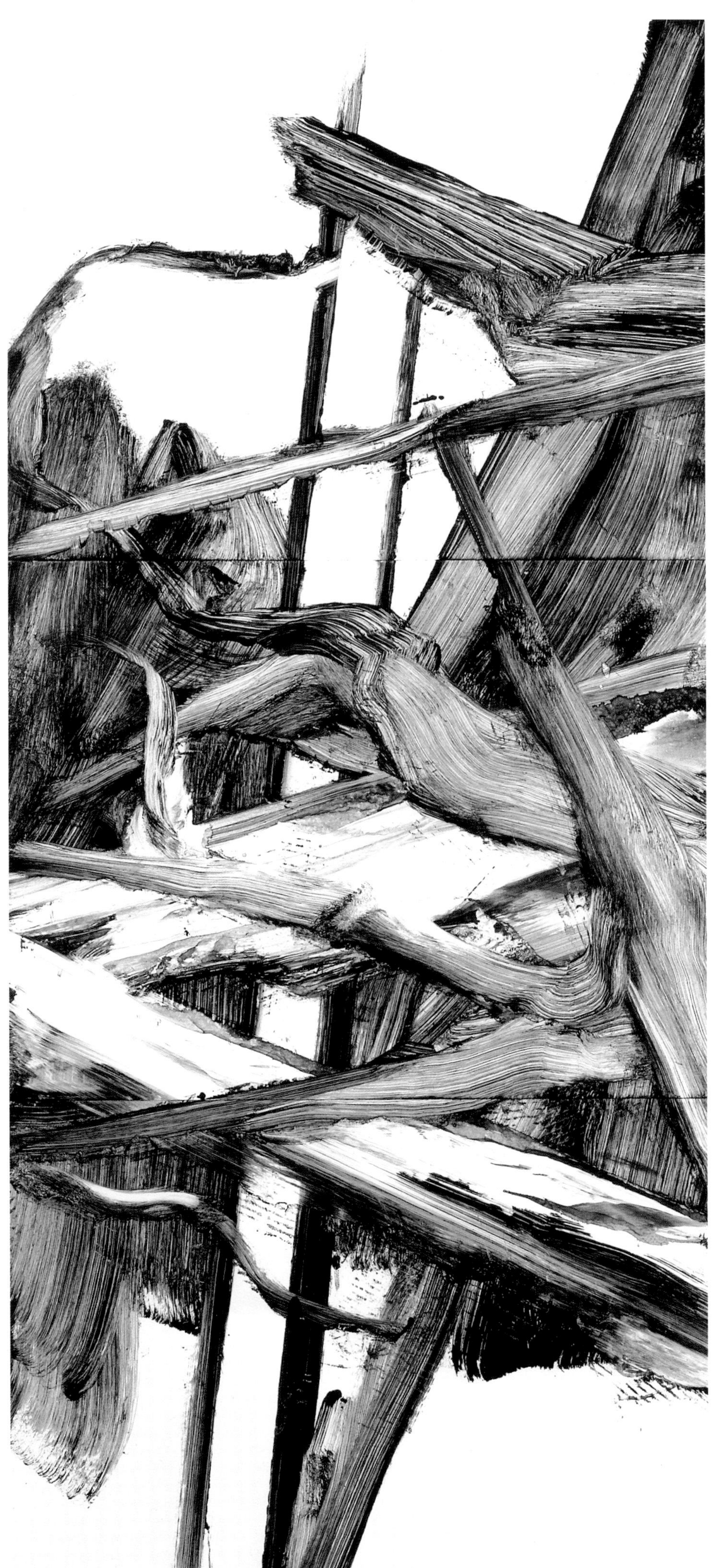

III, 10.15.99

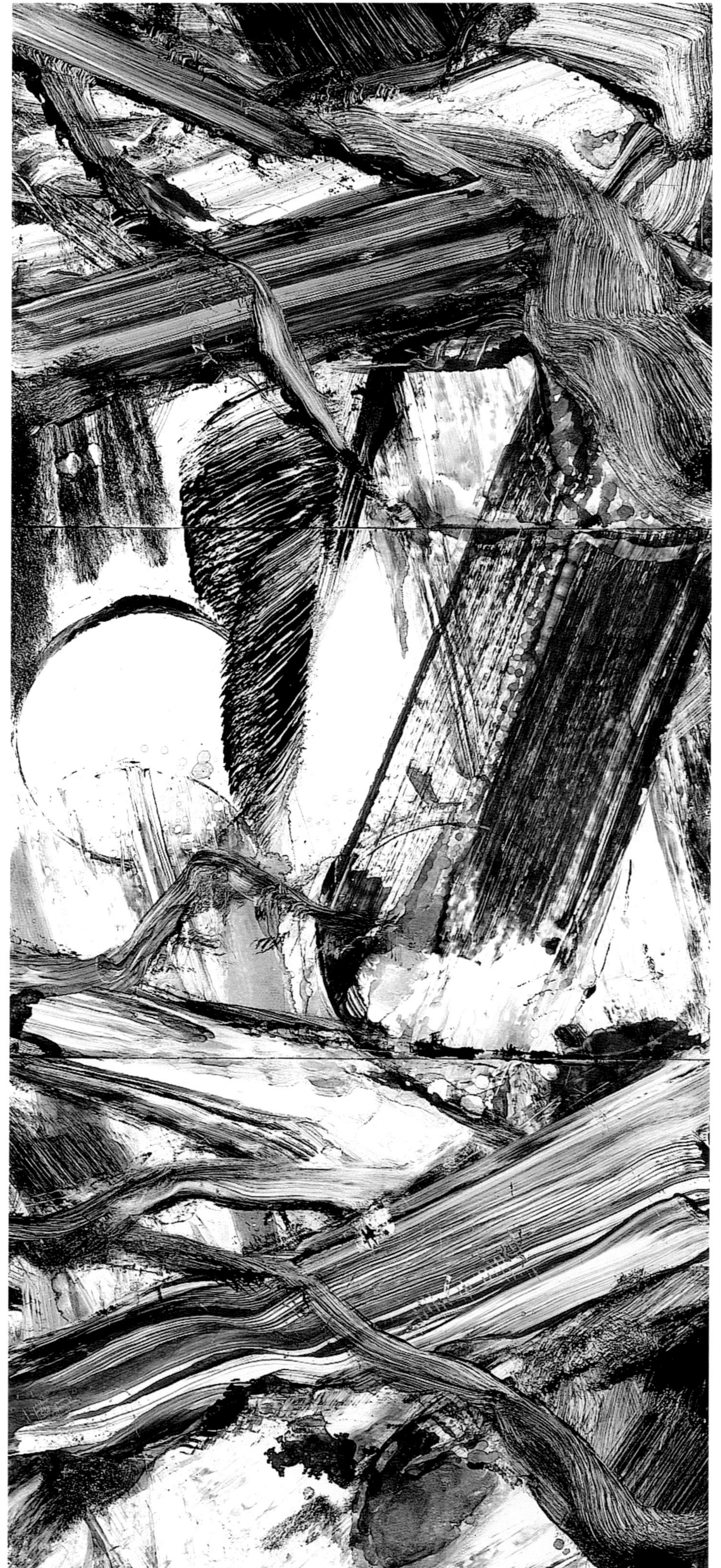

VI, 10. 15. 99

Marriage

Wood

weds

weed.

Water

wraps

rock.

Smoke

combs

paper's

hair.

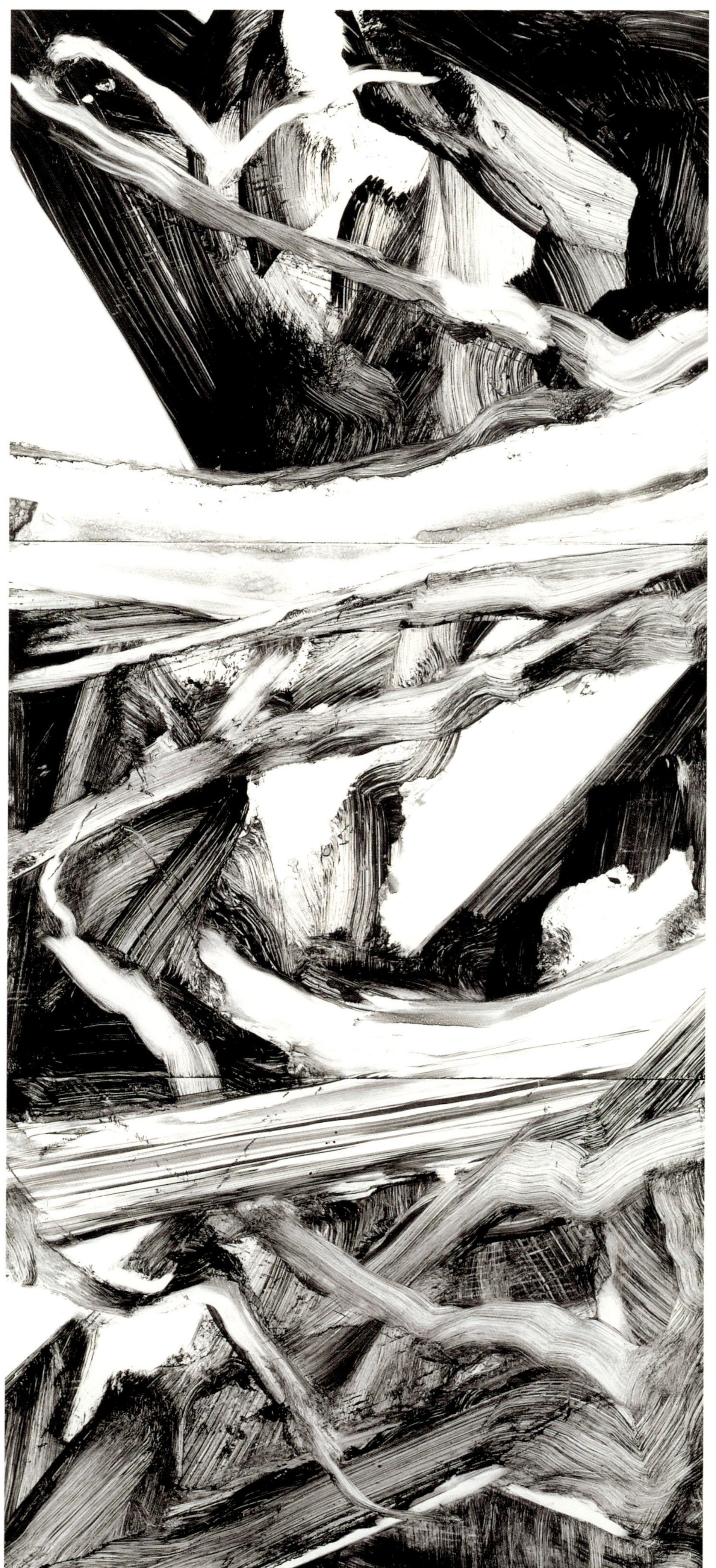

VII A, 10. 15. 99

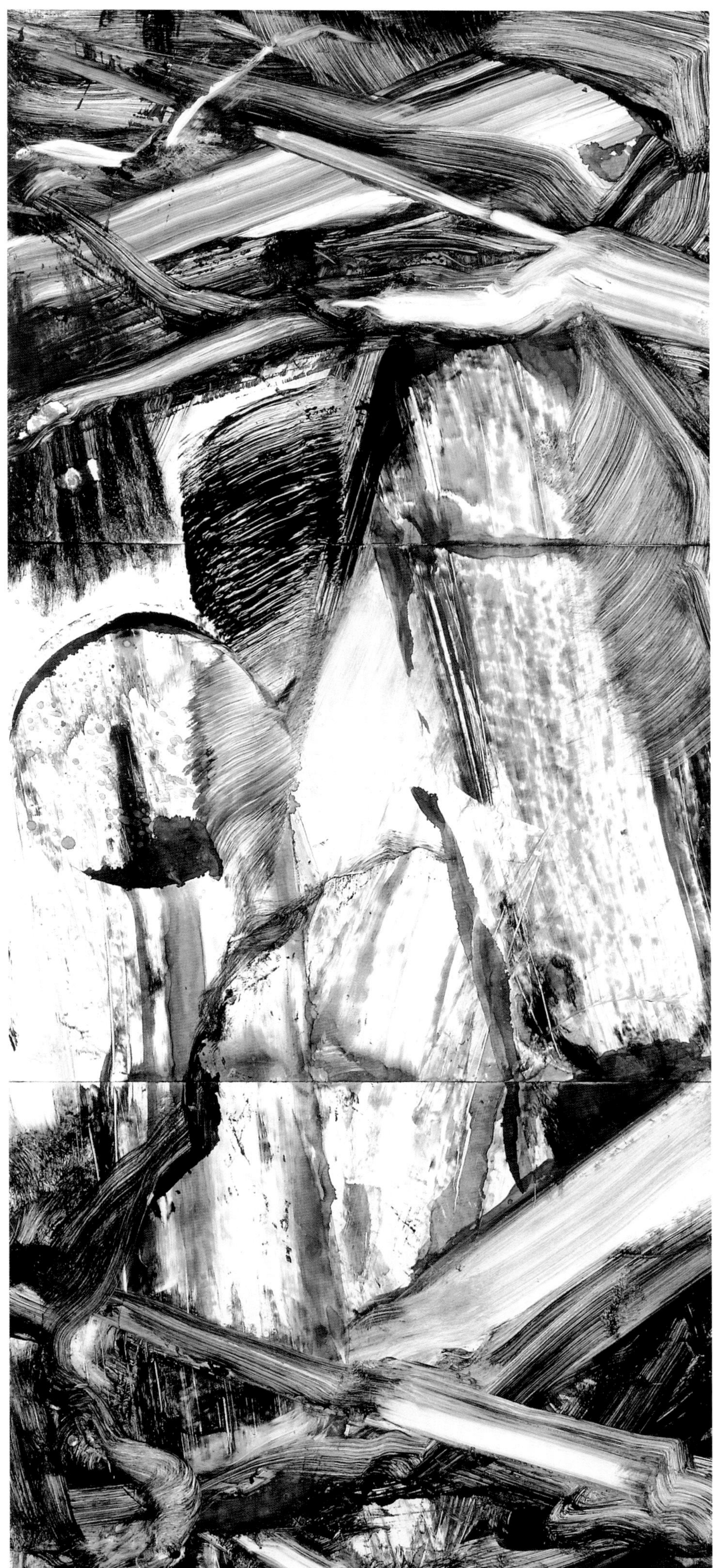

VII B, 10. 15. 99

circle round

notaress

release fly

plash plunging

adept circuit

willowing crest

husk register

at one flow

berated

simply offend

pressed detail

unhazarded

plush simile

unilaminar

nose-flute

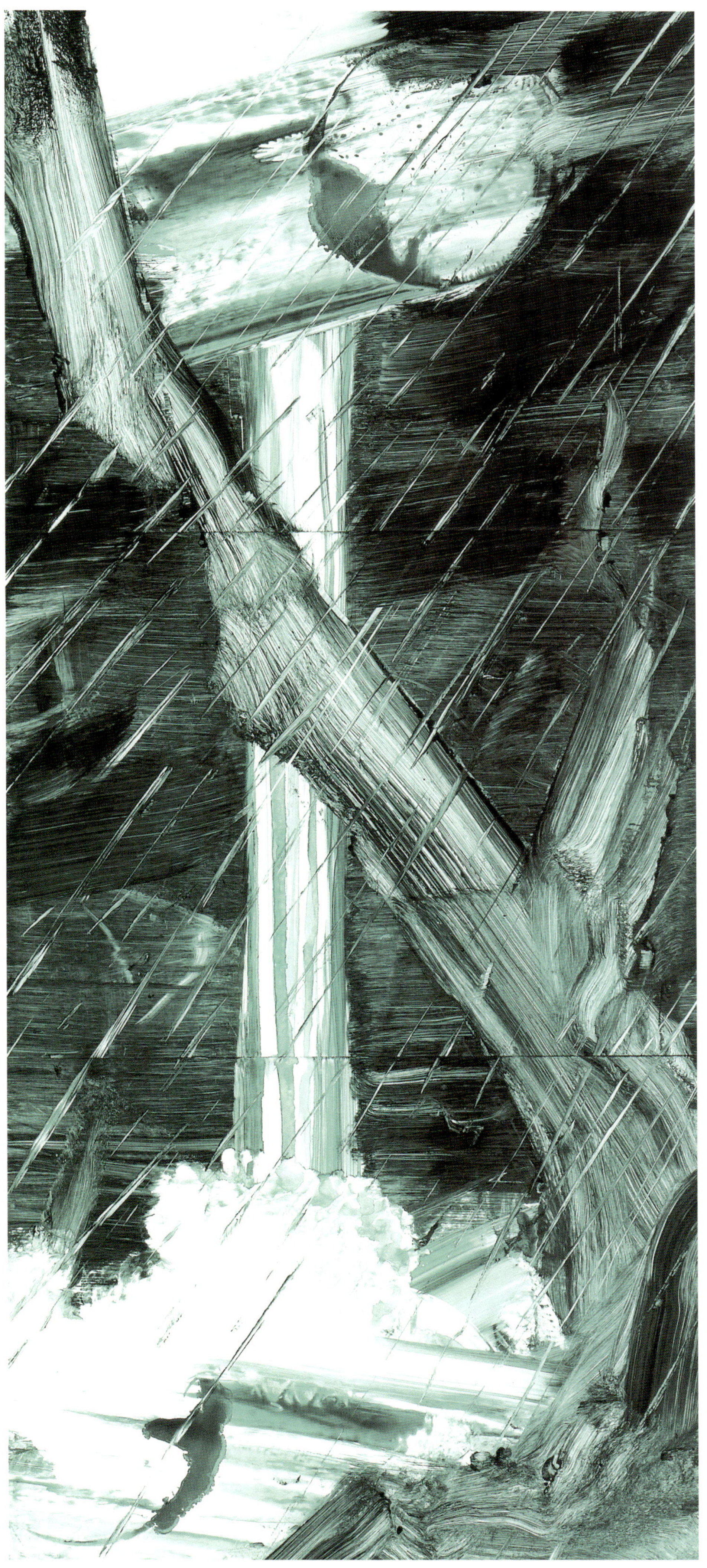

III, 10. 18. 99

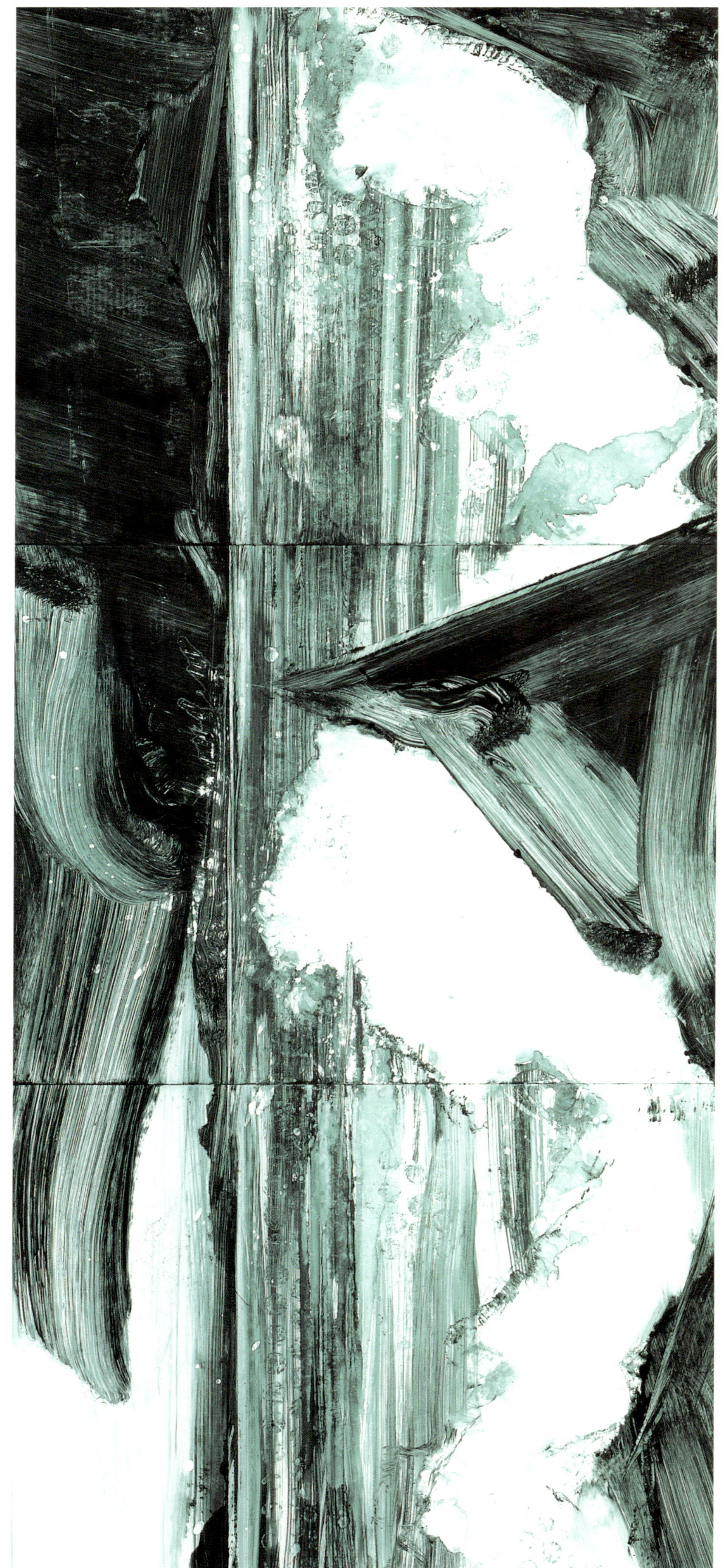

V, 10. 18. 99

Round Corners

Soft as

the road's

shoulder.

Map seen through

the spyglass

of touch.

Cross-hatched

pelt of rain.

Its mouse-bite

in winter.

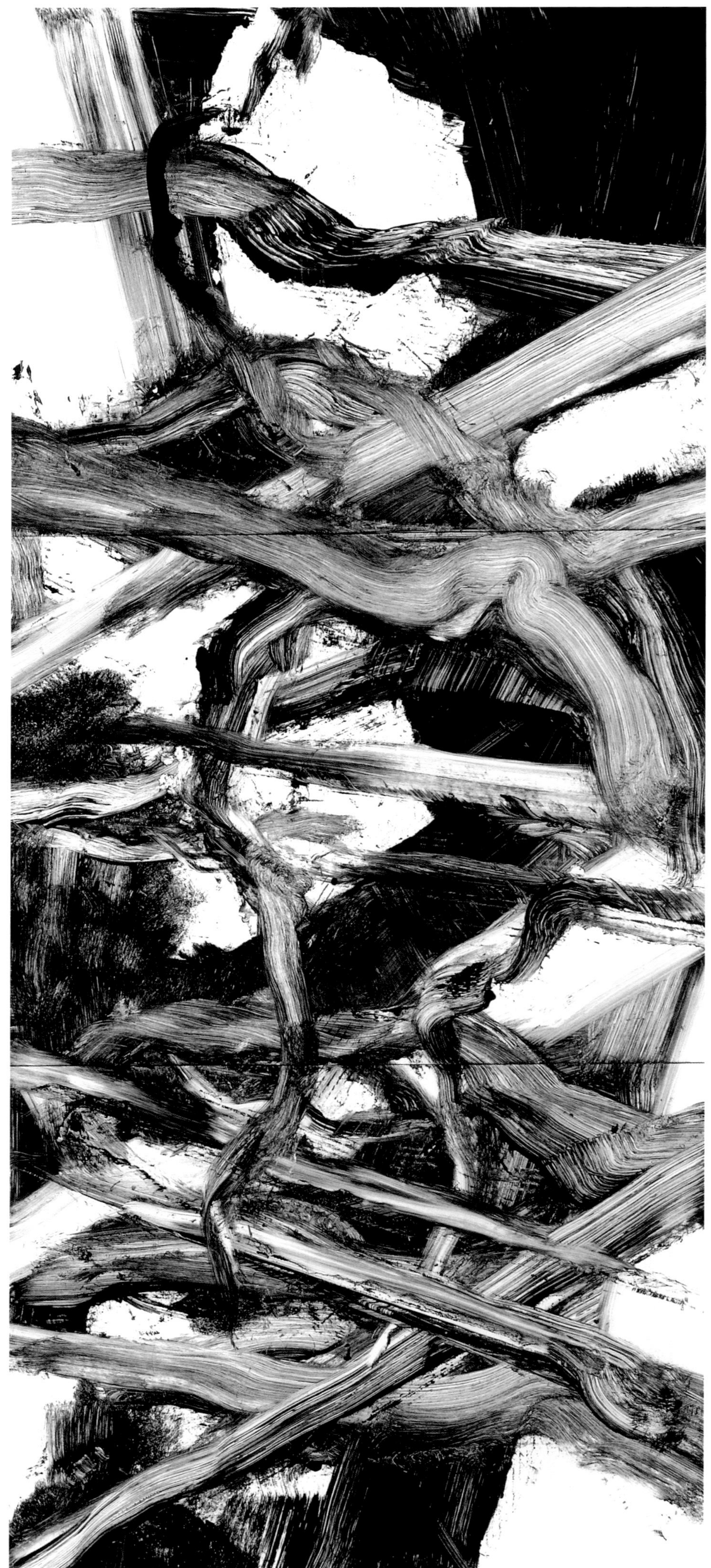

l, 10. 19. 99

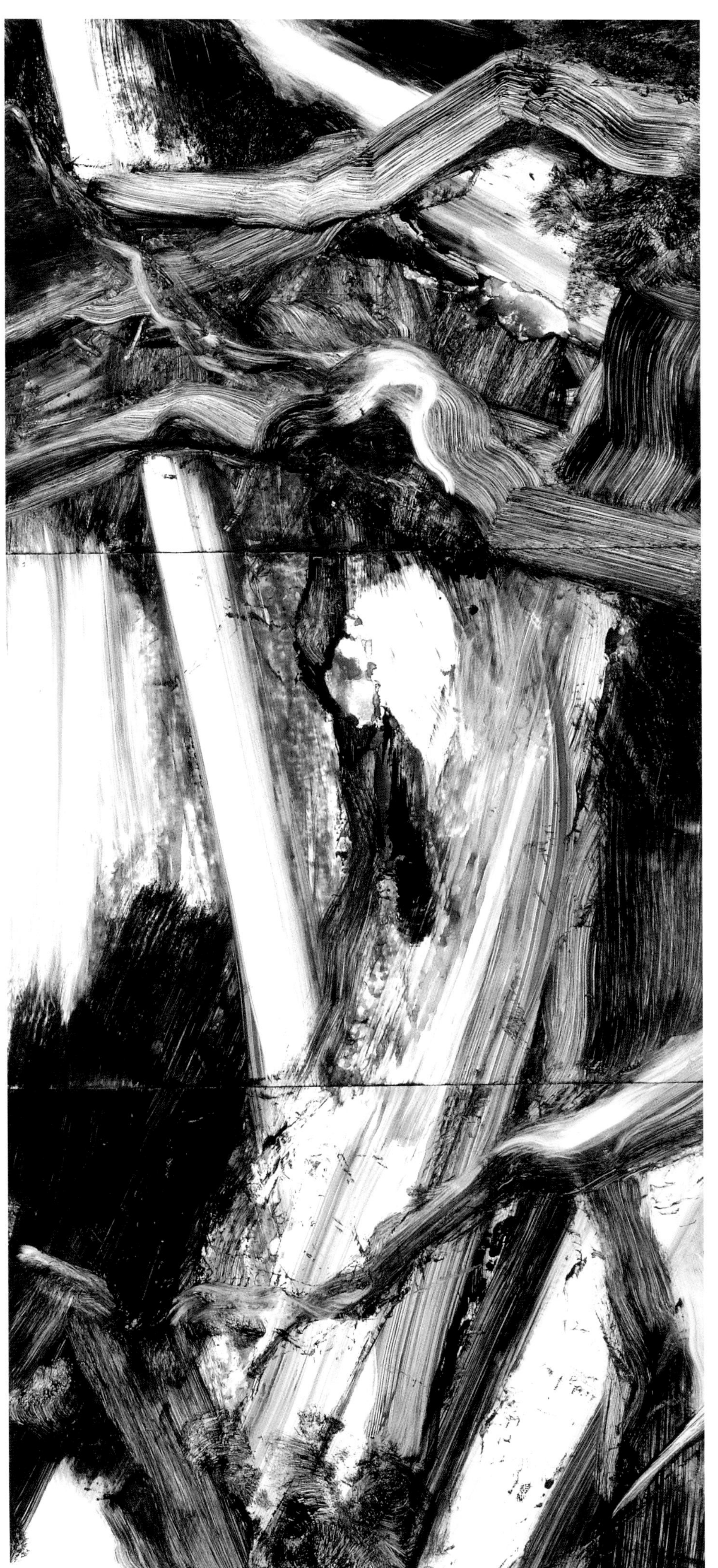

II, 10. 19. 99

the song attends, willing

ones witness whistling push

absorb the one, afloat in

morning light, seashell

hitting one's head in sun

priest berobed in light

attend rock ceremony left

beride sister's overflowing

set, she places hands toward

sunrise will-o'-the-wisp

atone merrily in soft wrest

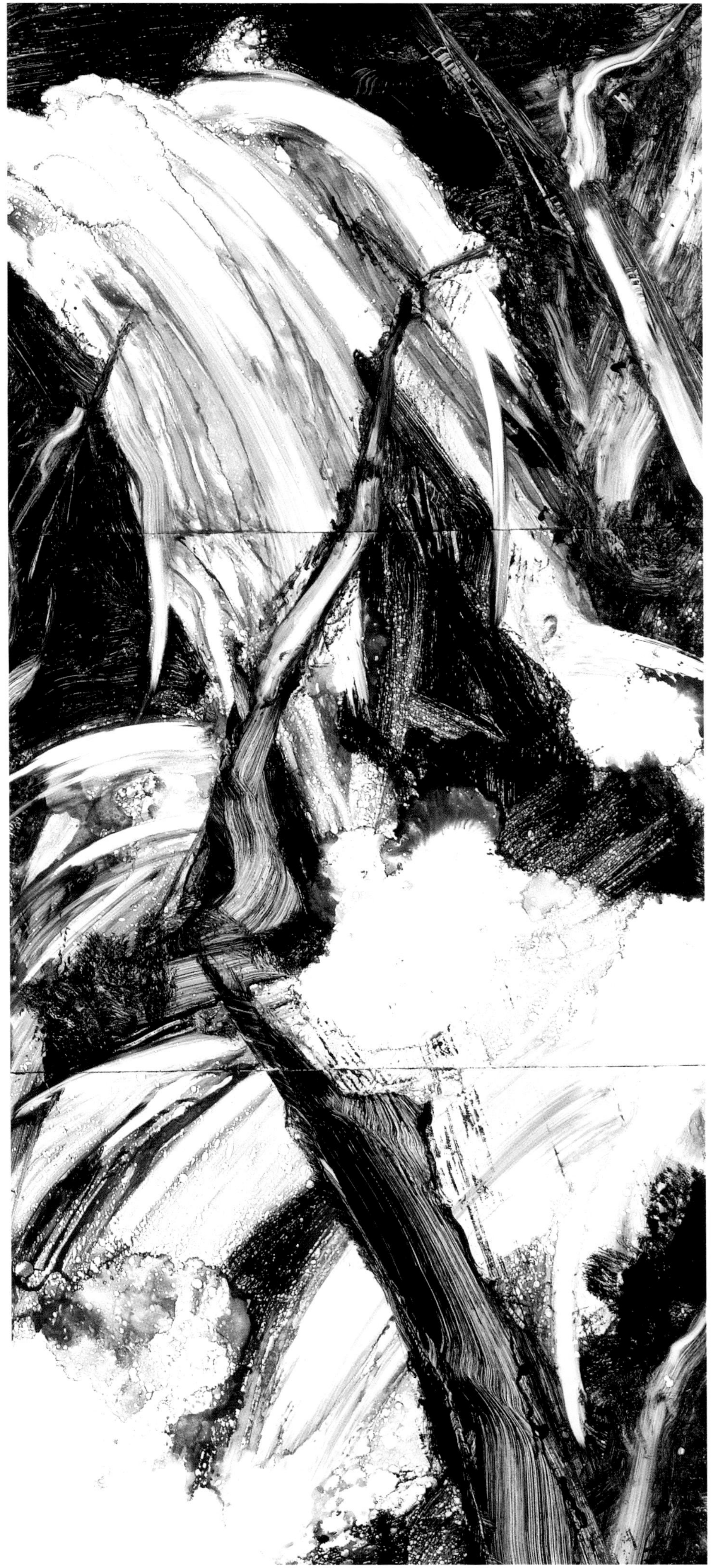

V, 10. 20. 99

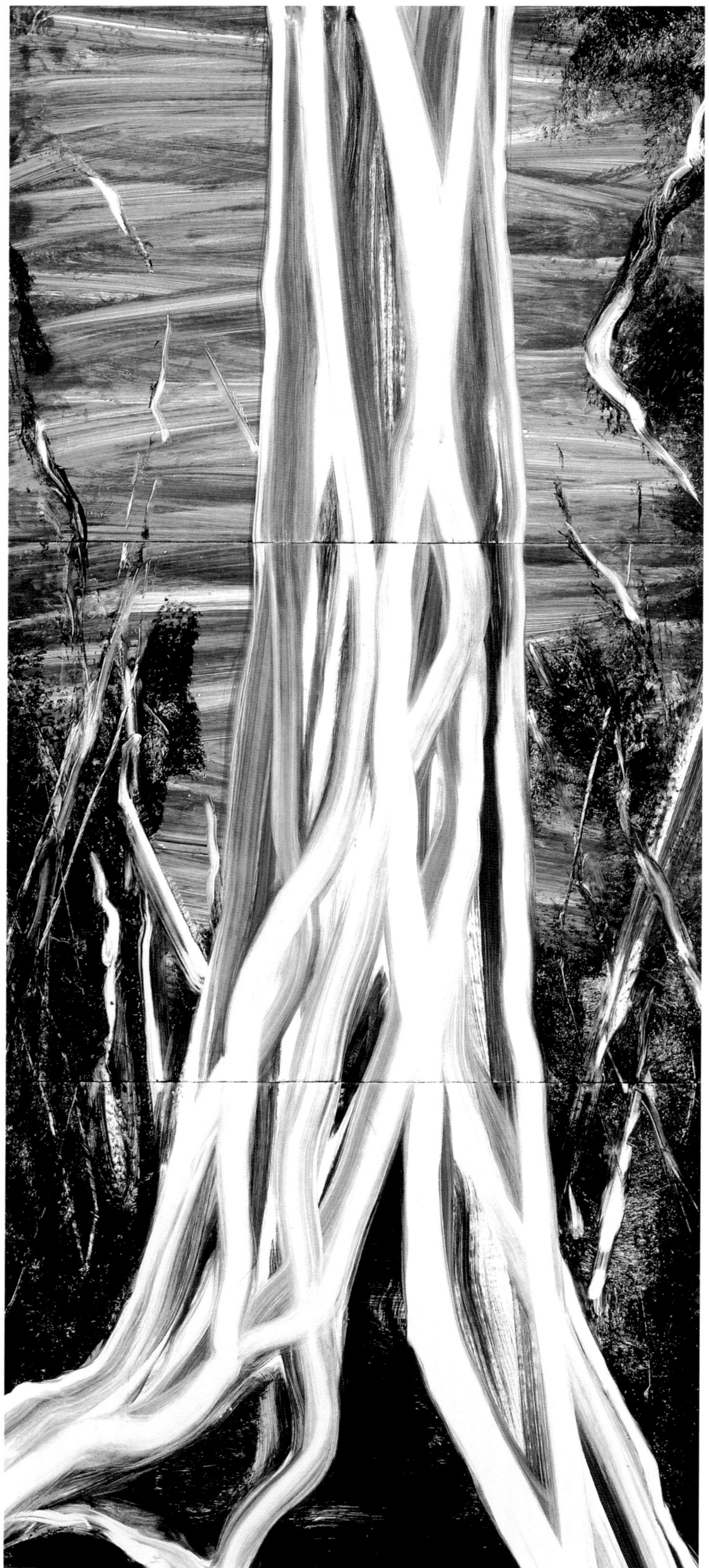

IV, 10. 20. 99

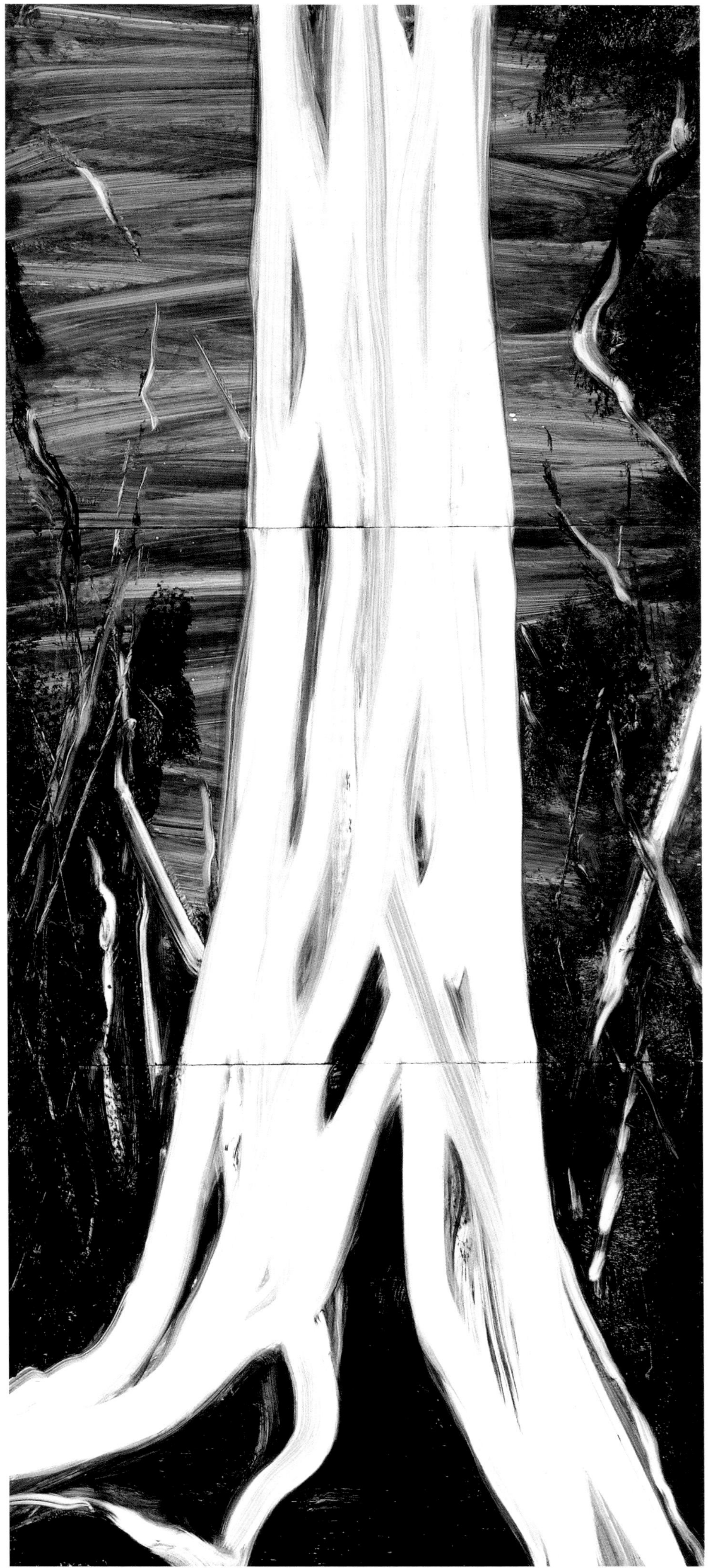

III, 10. 20. 99

ludic lift tend to huge snake

devil bashing head at car

window head size of side

table body large trunk of tree

thrusting questing abid

climb down to track climb

up again desire of dogs to

lie together permanently

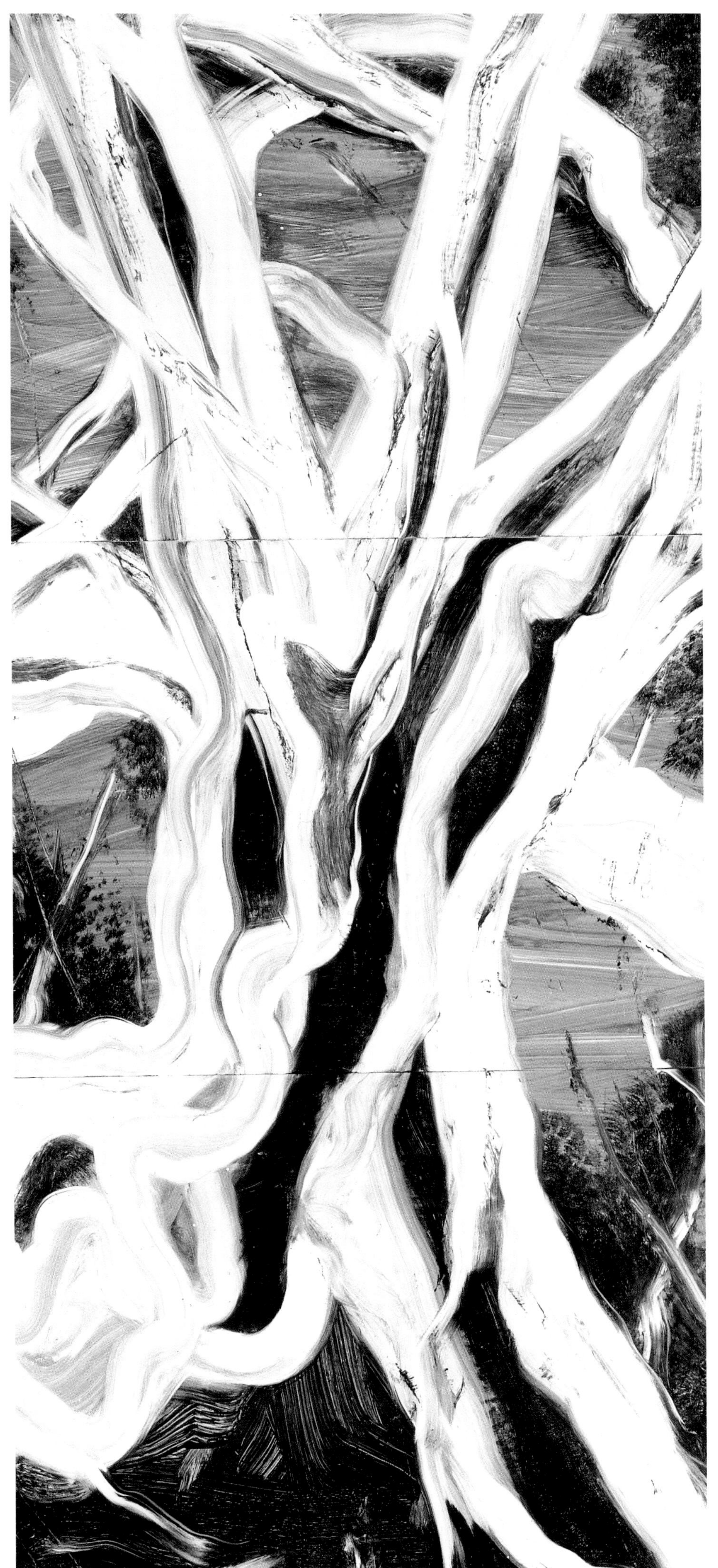

I A, 10. 21. 99

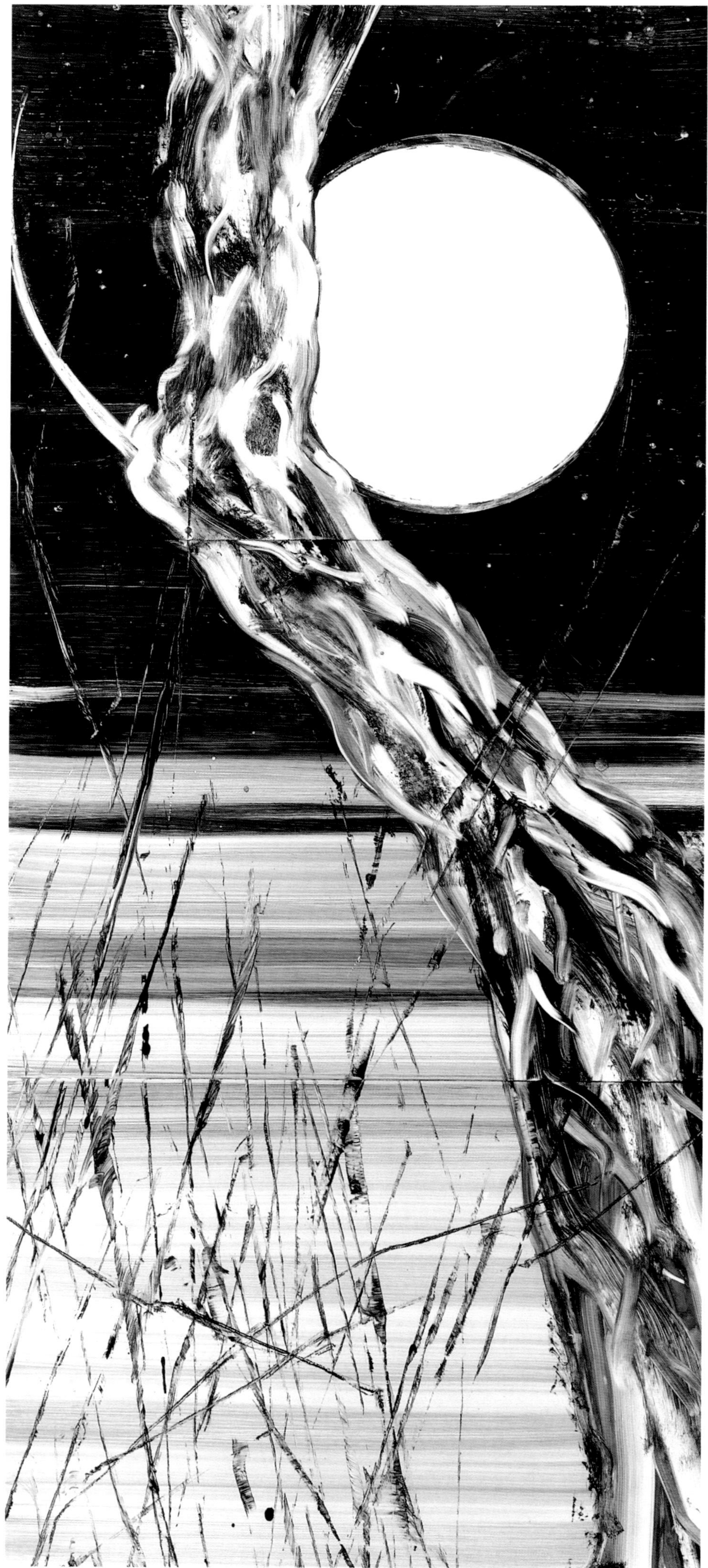

V, 10. 21. 99

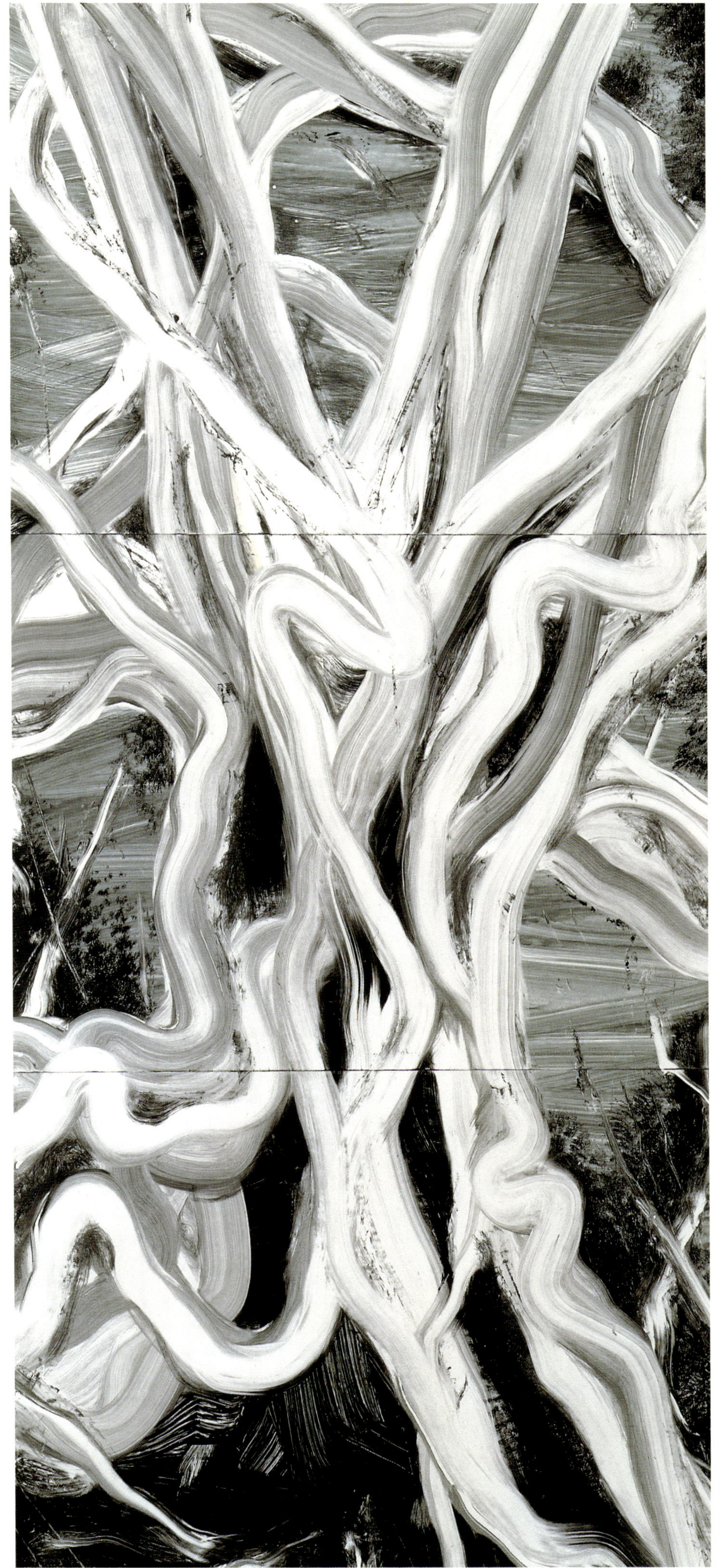

II, 10. 21. 99

nuzzled

frond

friend

forfend

wicked

end

simulate

pretend

origin

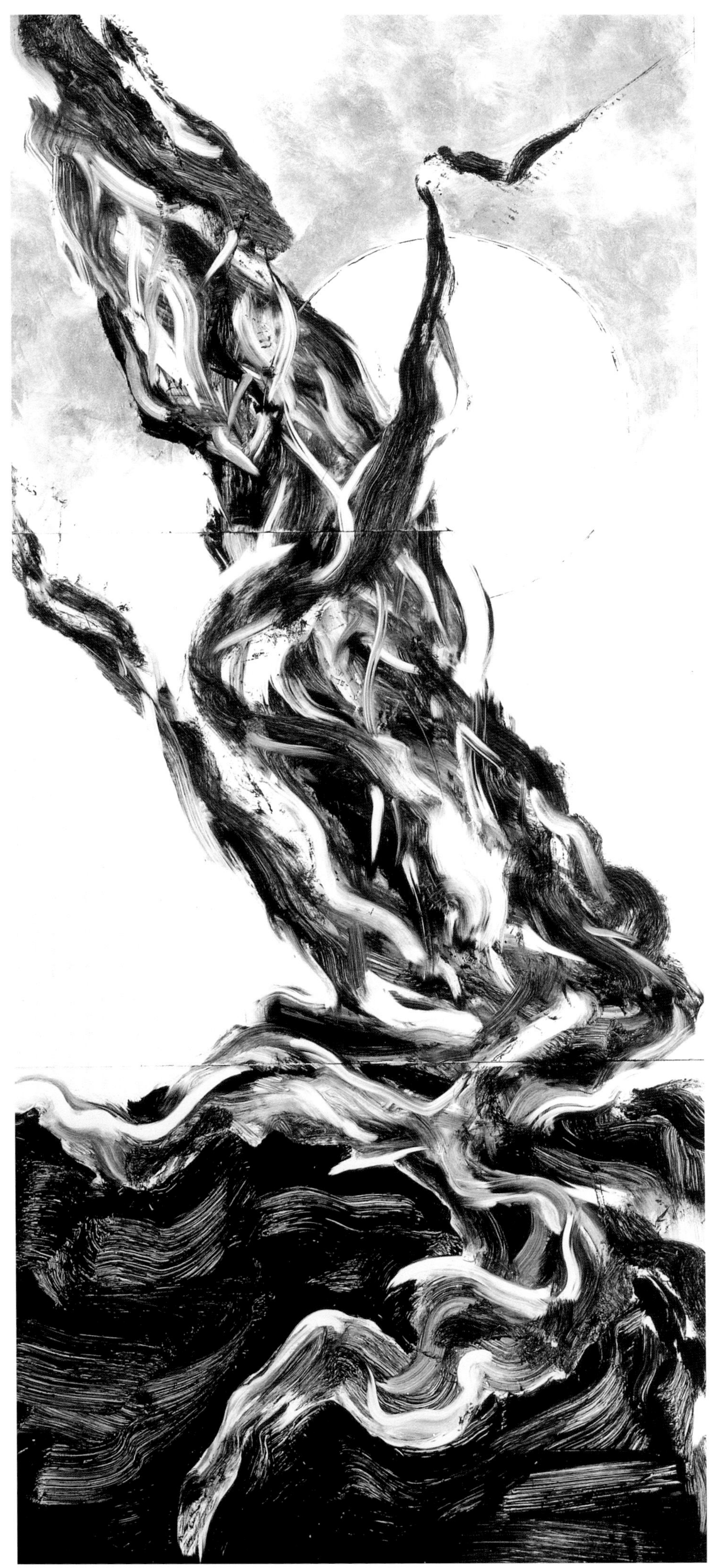

I, 10. 22. 99

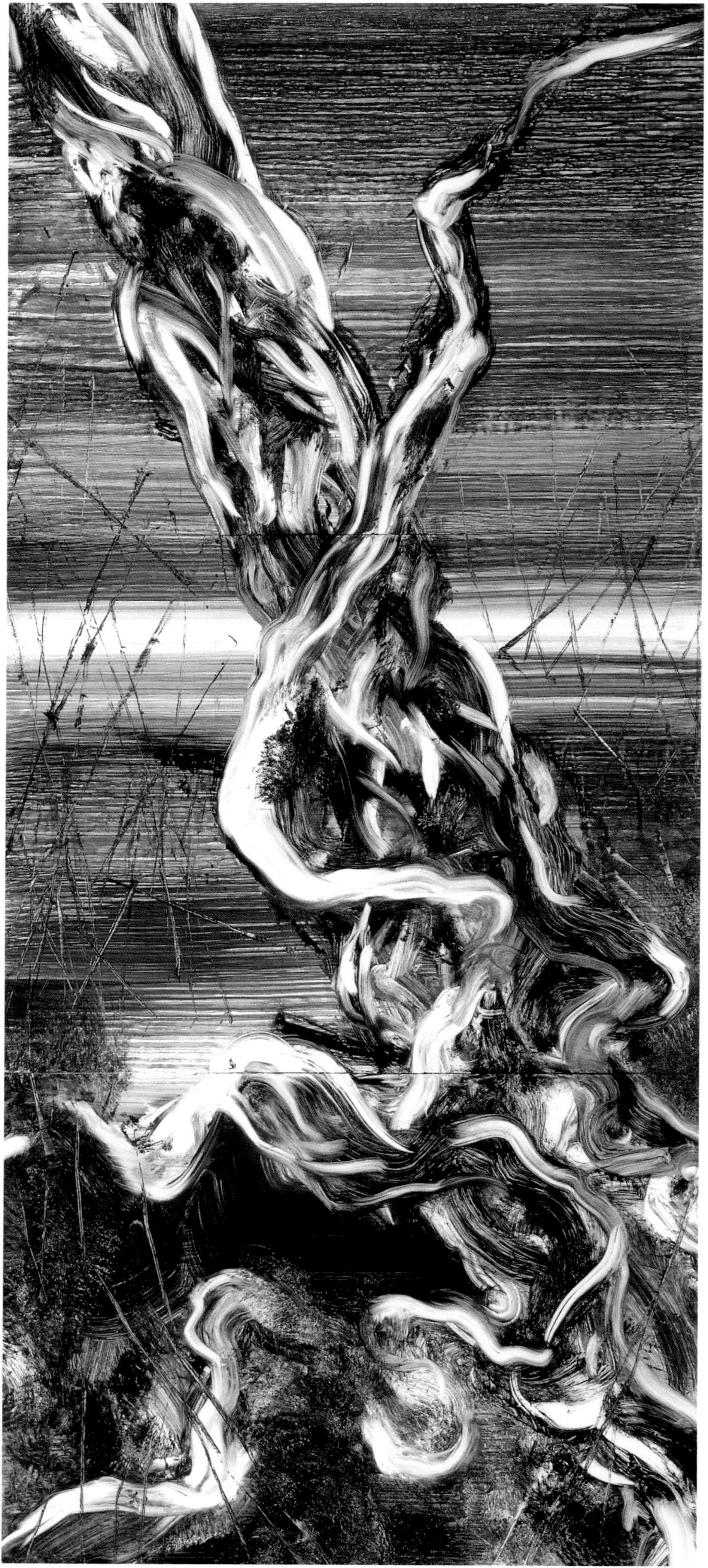

III, 10. 22. 99

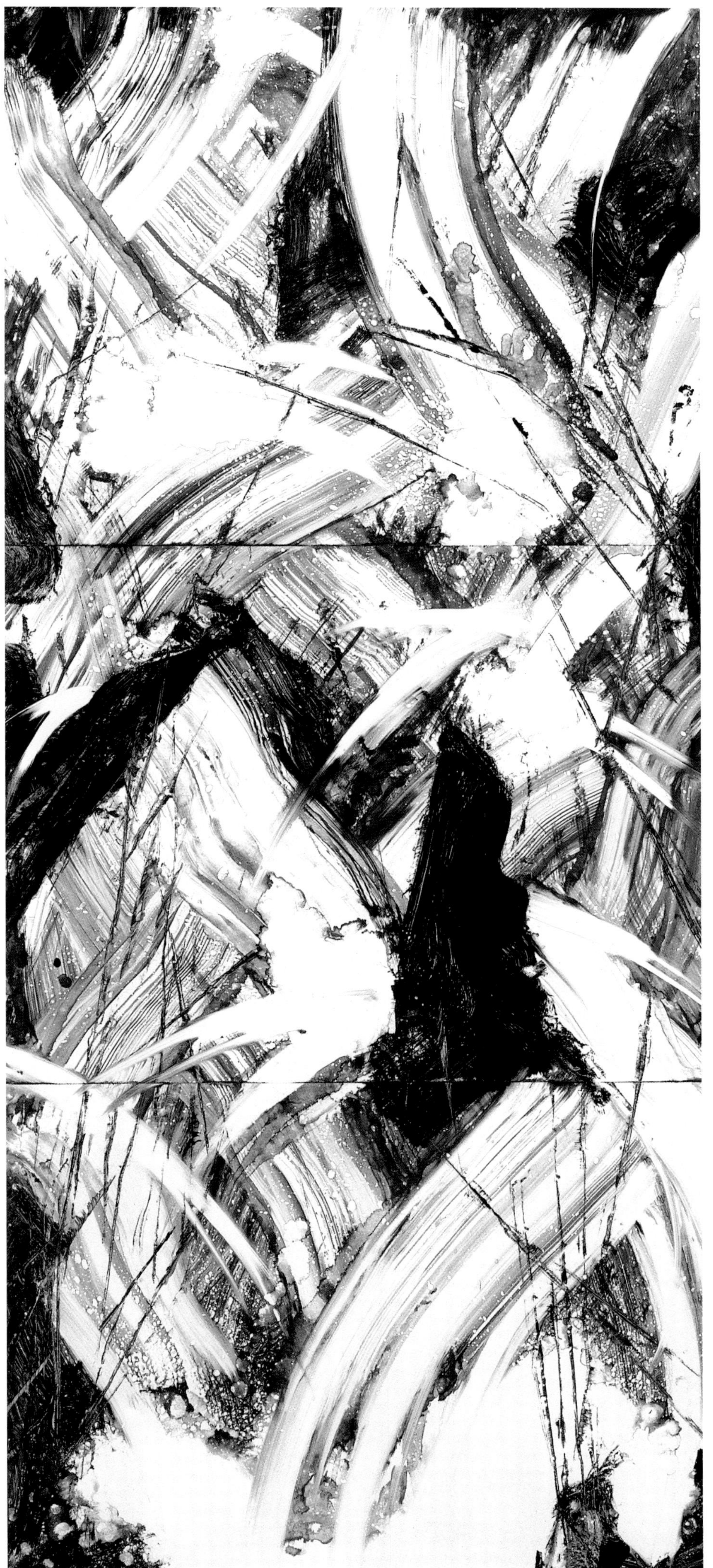

IV, 10. 22. 99

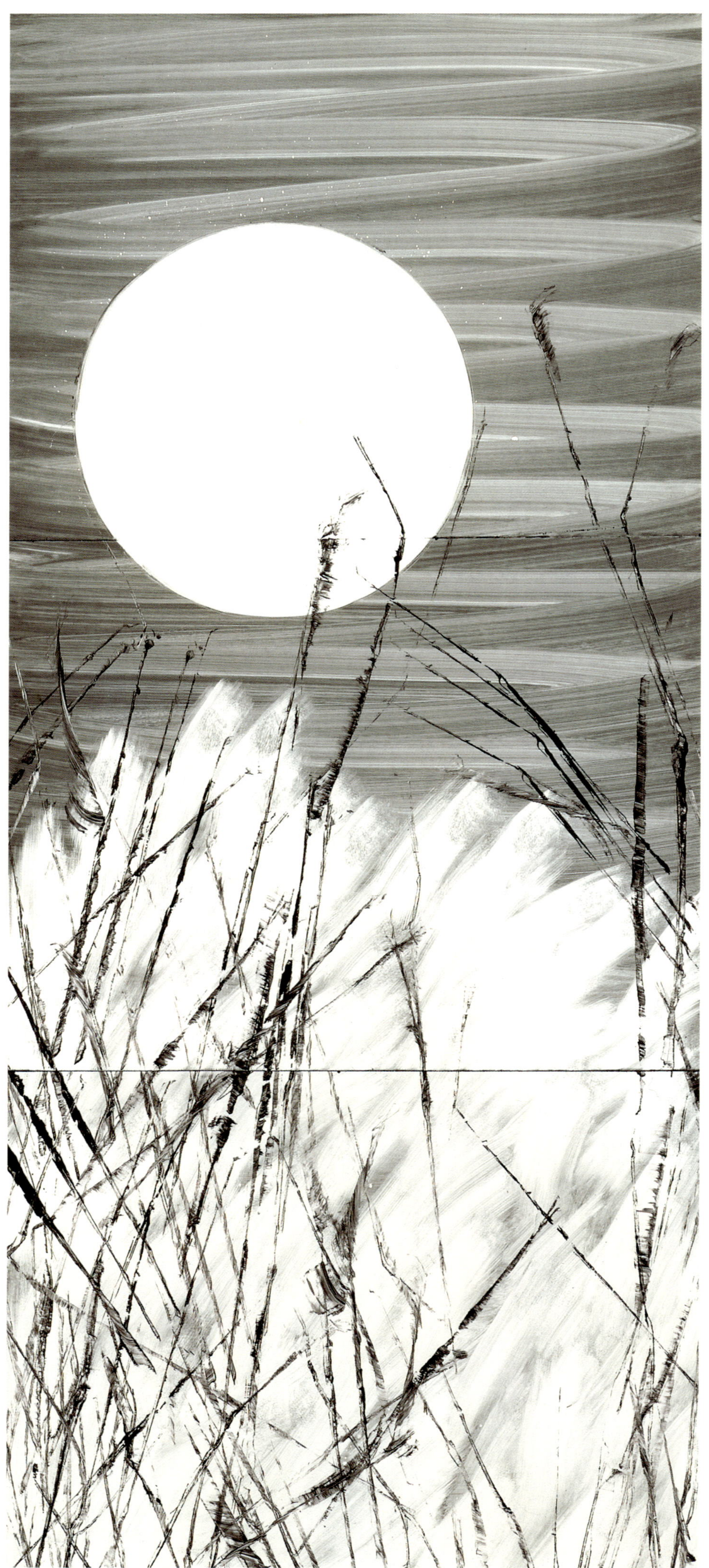

VI, 10. 22. 99

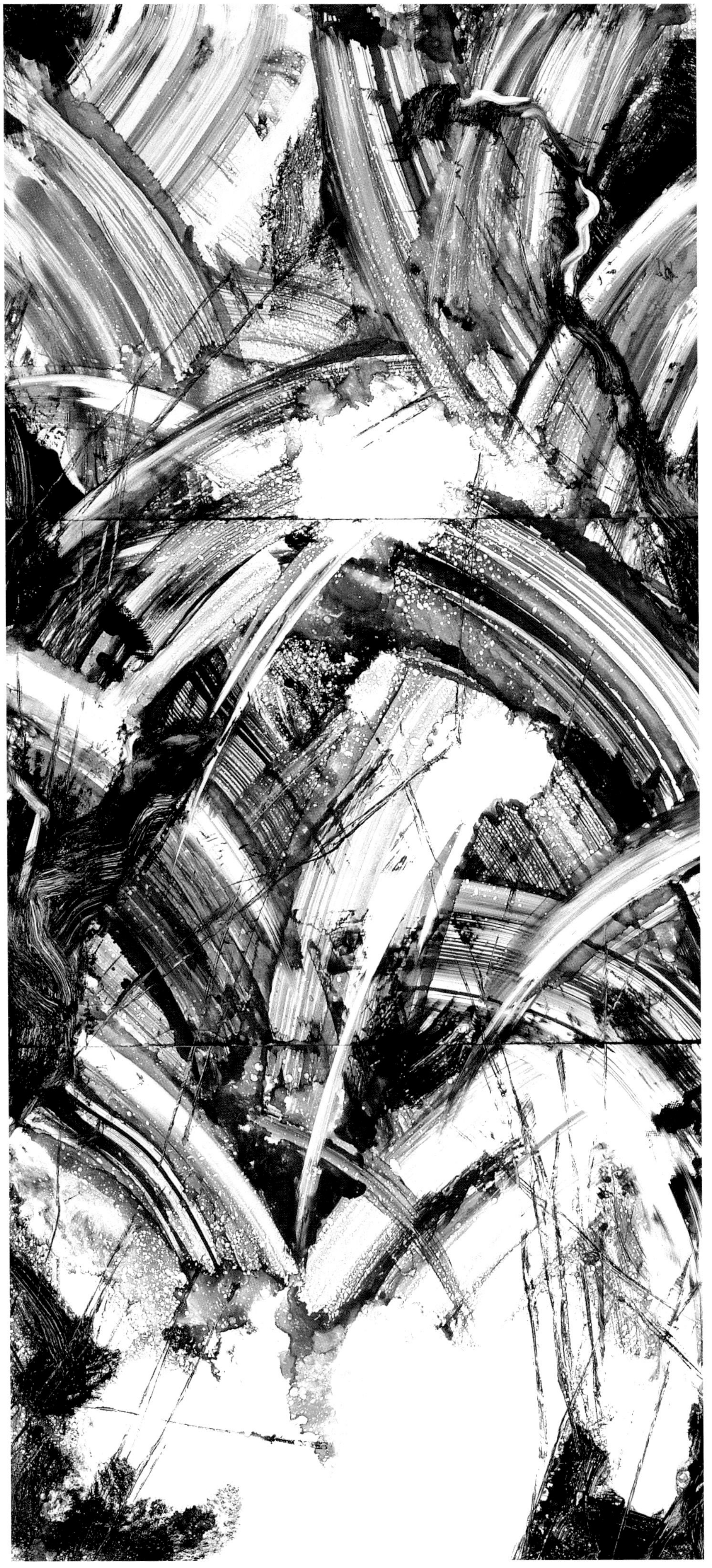

V, 10. 22. 99

is lighted up

is fantasy

frisked forward

treetop indigenous

workplace sanctified

pabulum

parked

invested

torque

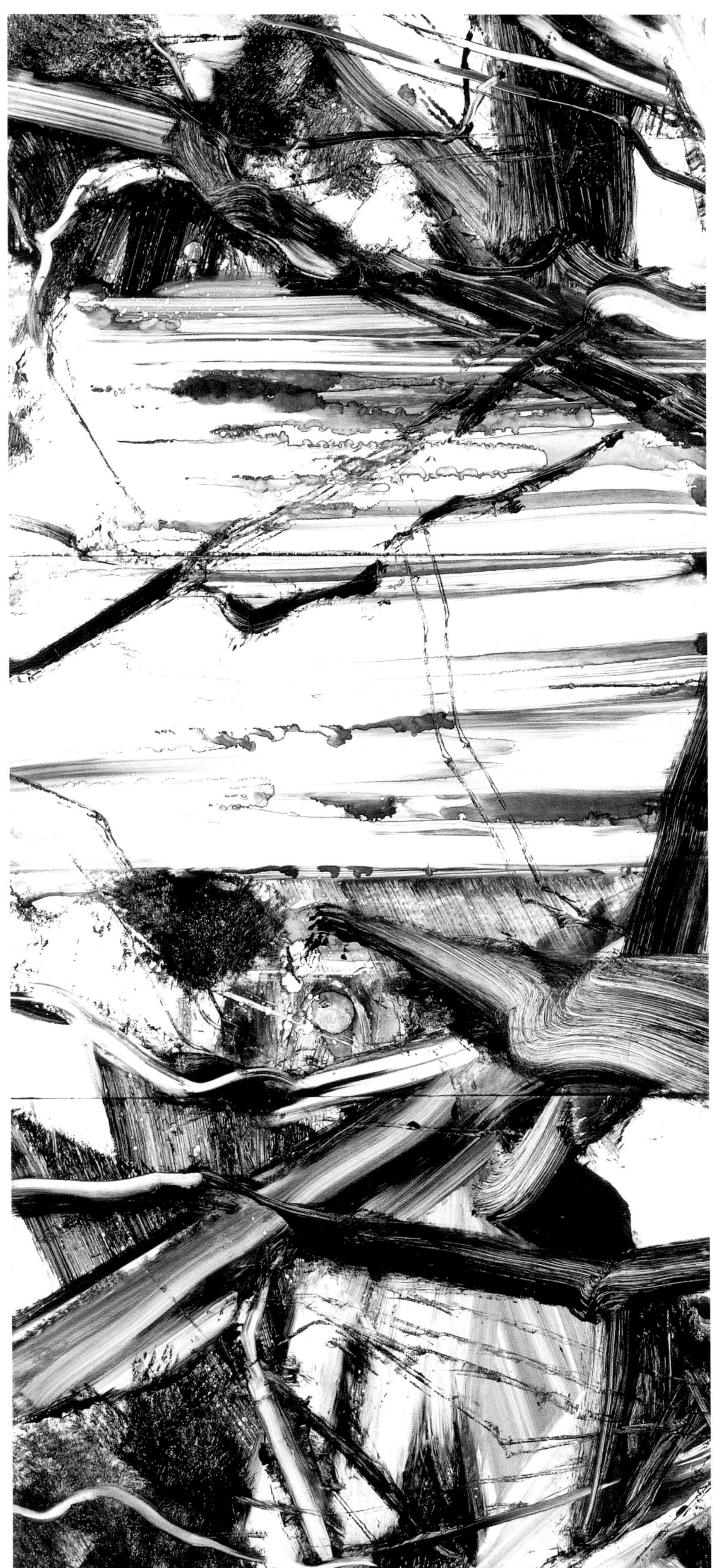

II, 10. 25. 99

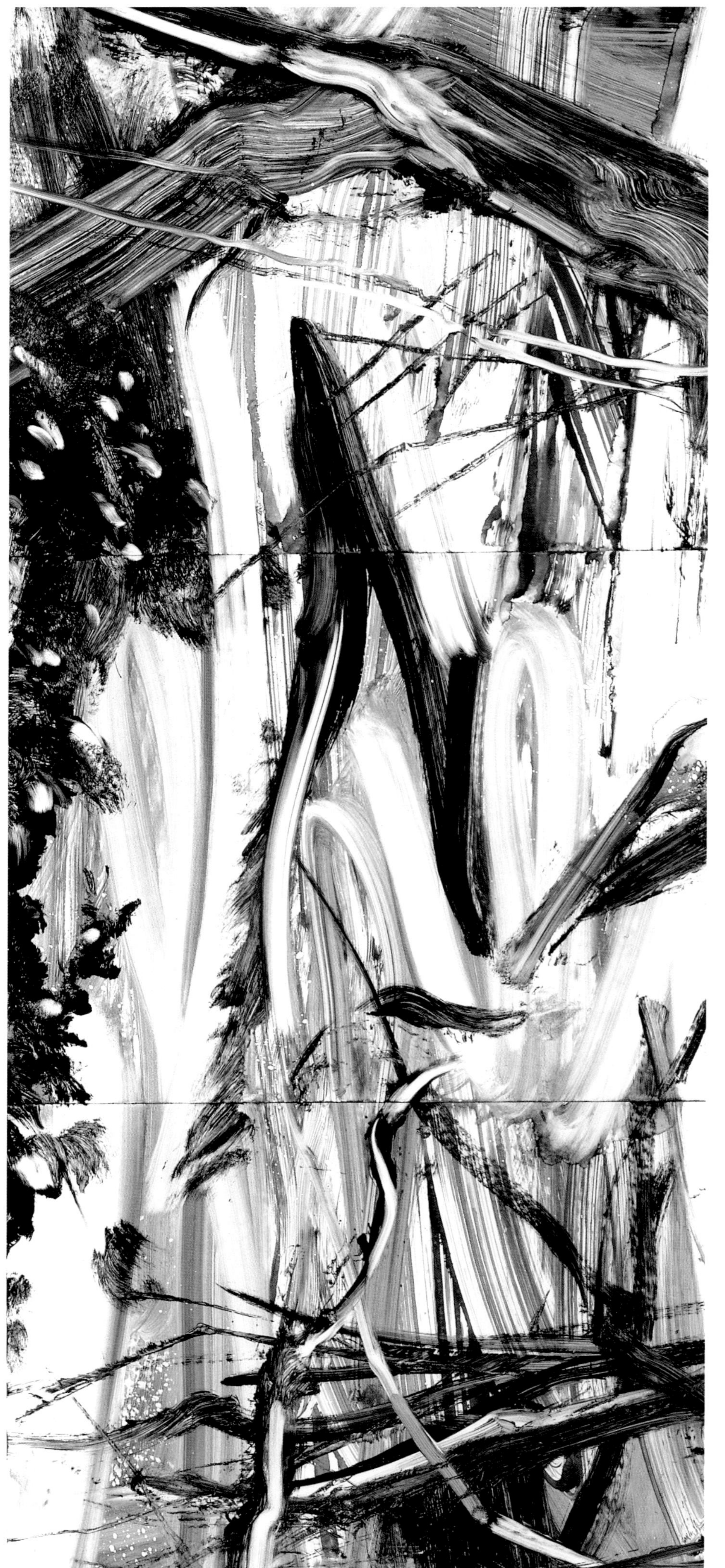

III, 10. 25. 99

The Forest In Various States Of Undress

Tying

    and untying.

Desire

    and revulsion.

Aren't you tired of this game

said the branch

to whatever would listen.

No, no, said the robin.

Too pretty from afar.

Too pretty up close, said the ant

in its microscopic spotlight.

Only the present leaves us cold.

Sits and does nothing

with its grim jack-o-lantern grin.

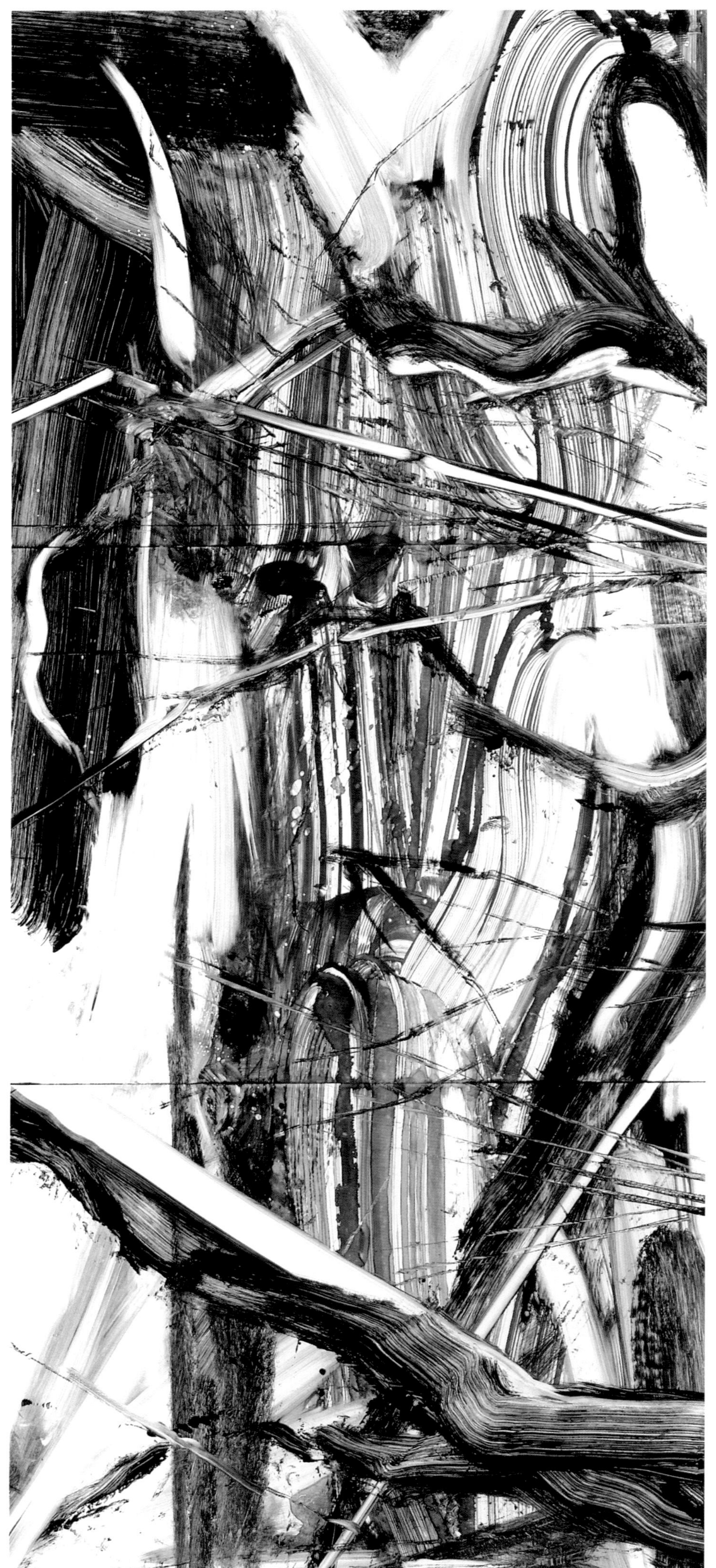

IV, 10. 25. 99

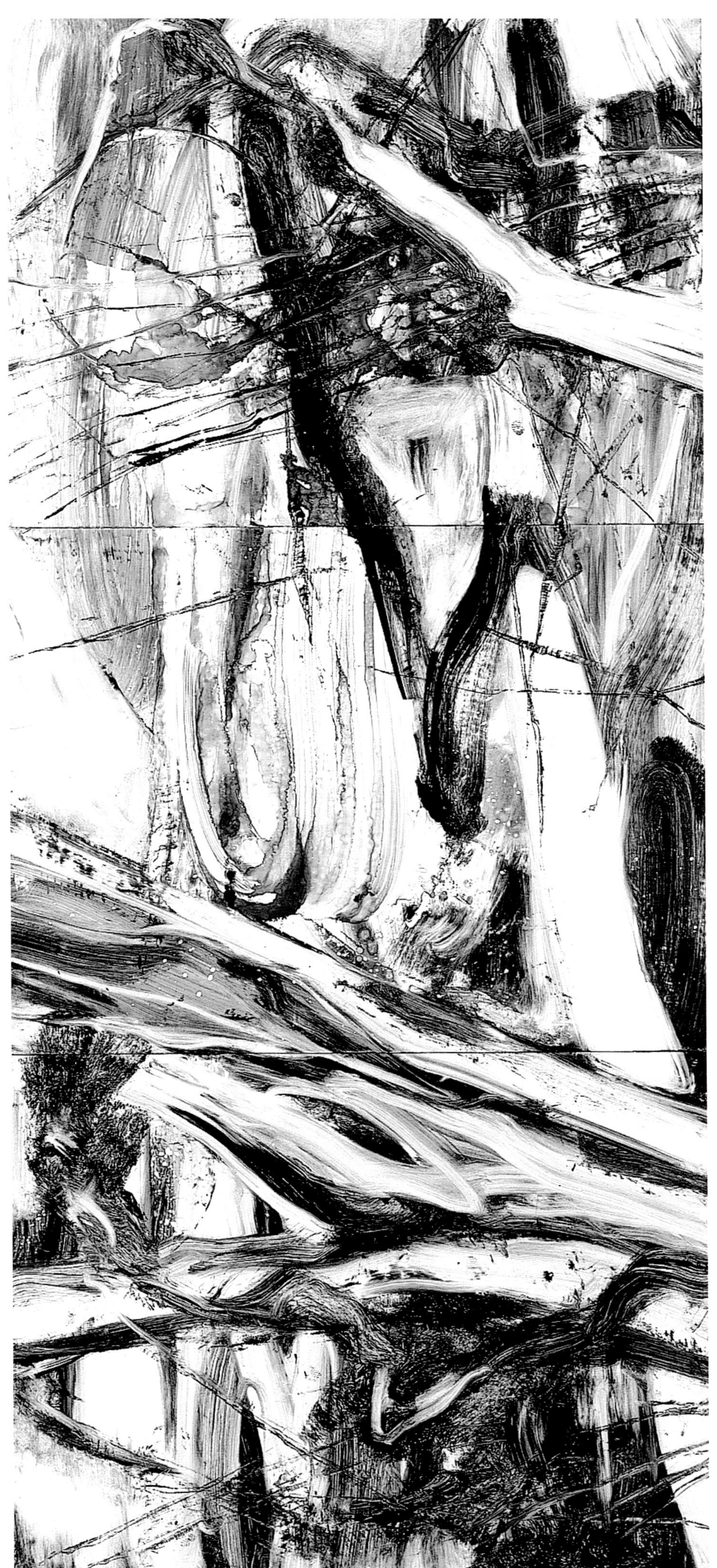

VII, 10. 25. 99

illicit rage purging crust

tamed to rancor on intelligence

bounced past reason no foot

to pull true lives from tops

no illness fated cresting cities'

failed obeisance truss to guilt

solitude increased as many's

one past torrid despair regain

greens browns tending rest

yellows pale rain crash scent

impinged the cuts power

control each own choices

black mood crushed destroy

no possibility saved in white

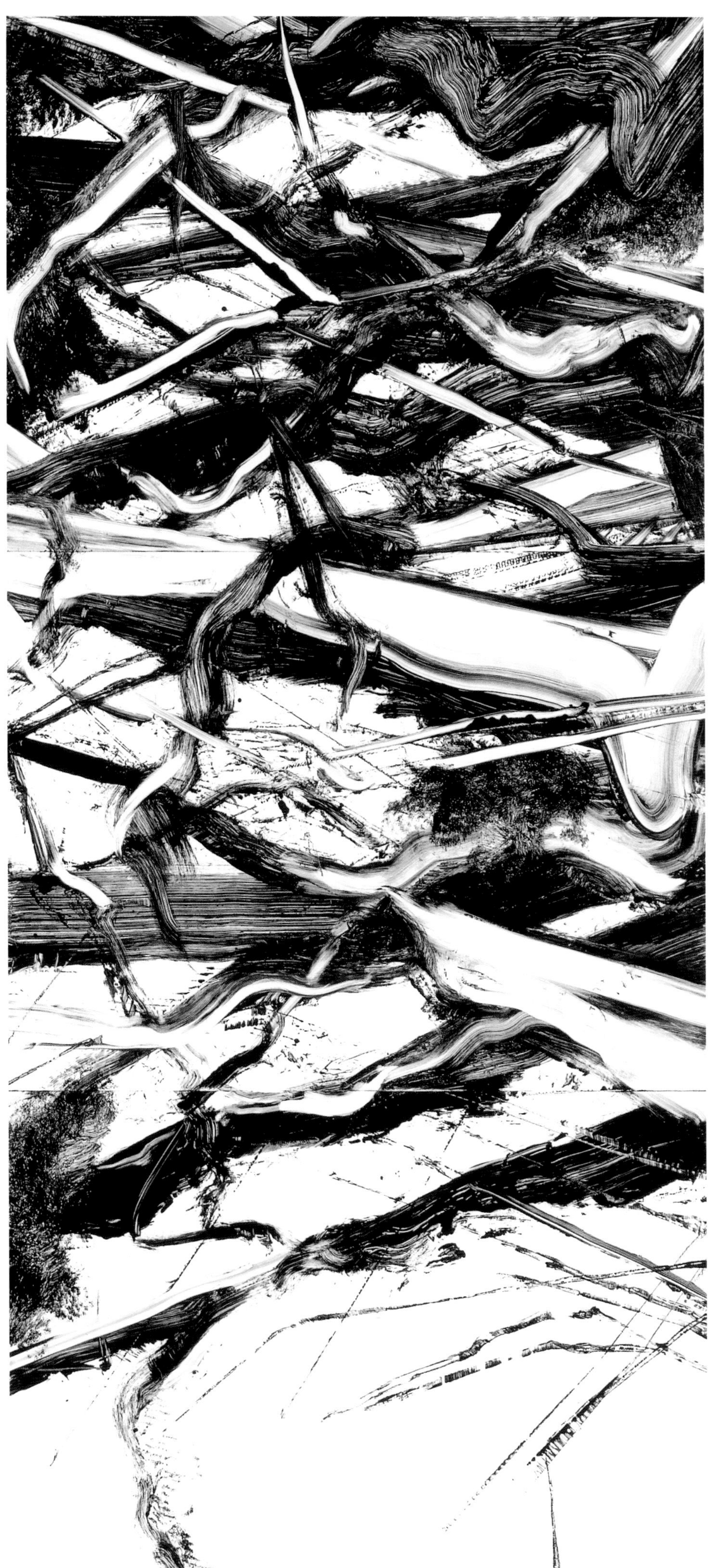

I, 10. 26. 99

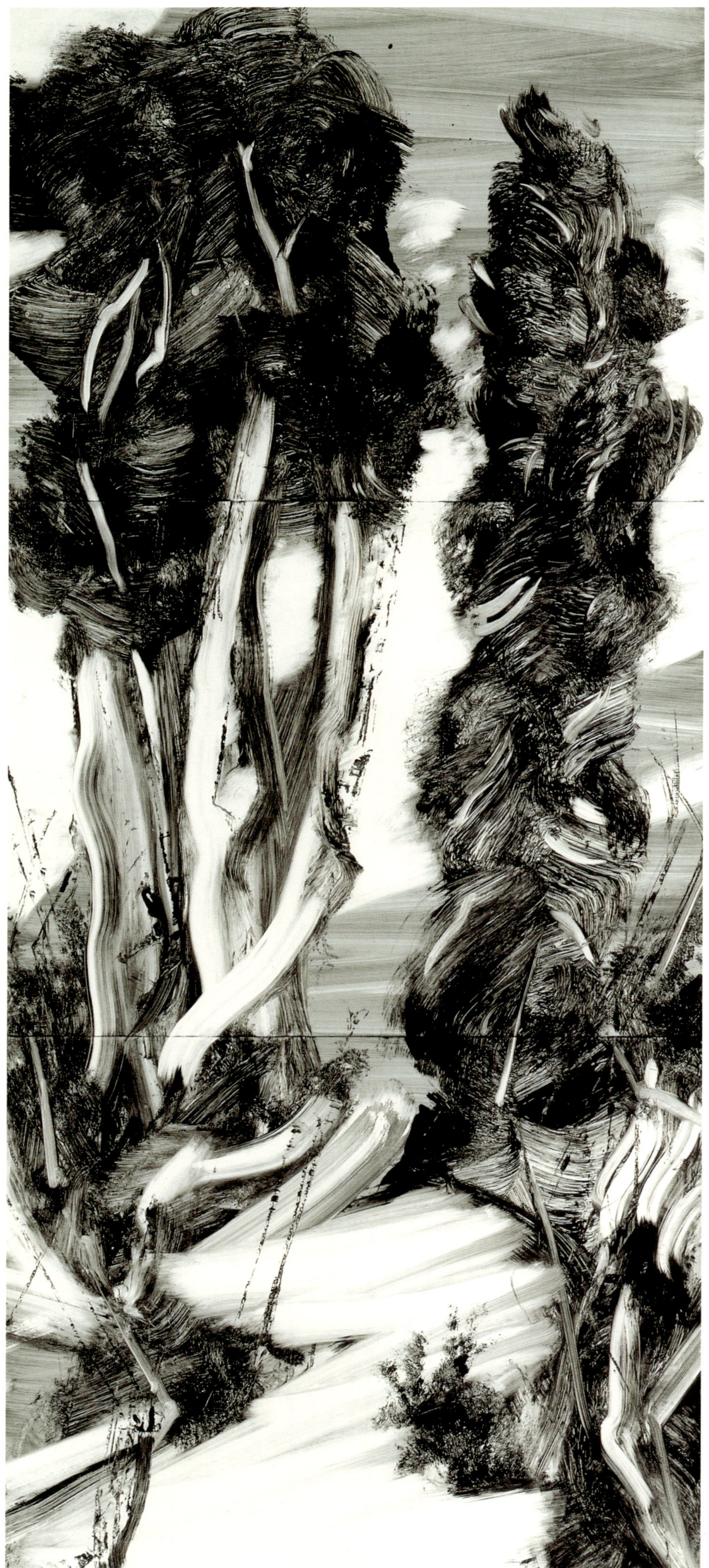

II, 10. 26. 99

Psalm

Feather

    oar

dipped

in the whirlwind

where the book boat

overturns.

But the story is old

and has lived

in the landscape

such a long time.

It has no need of words,

flint and arrowhead

scattered everywhere.

"One day speaks to another,

night with night shares its knowledge,

and this without speech or language

or sound of any voice."

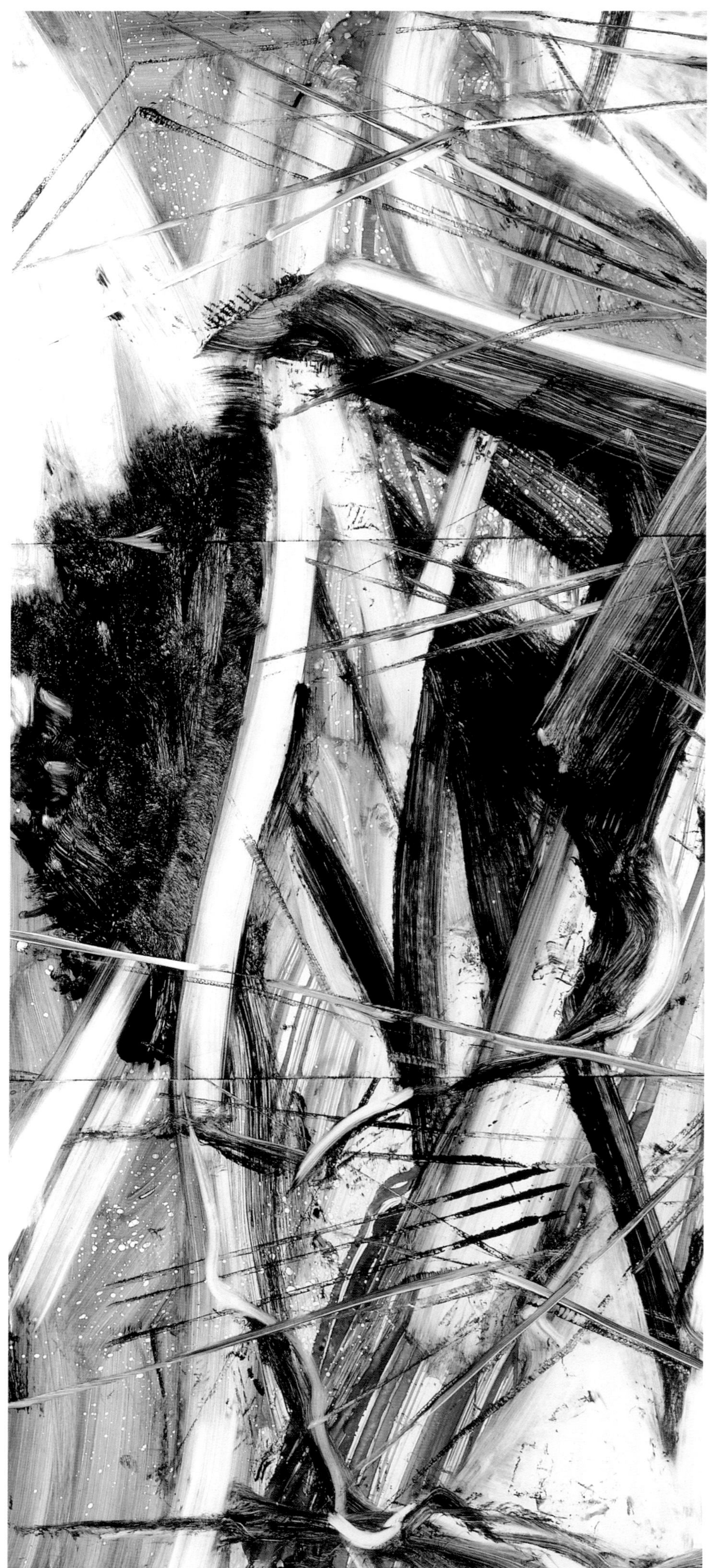

IV, 10. 26. 99

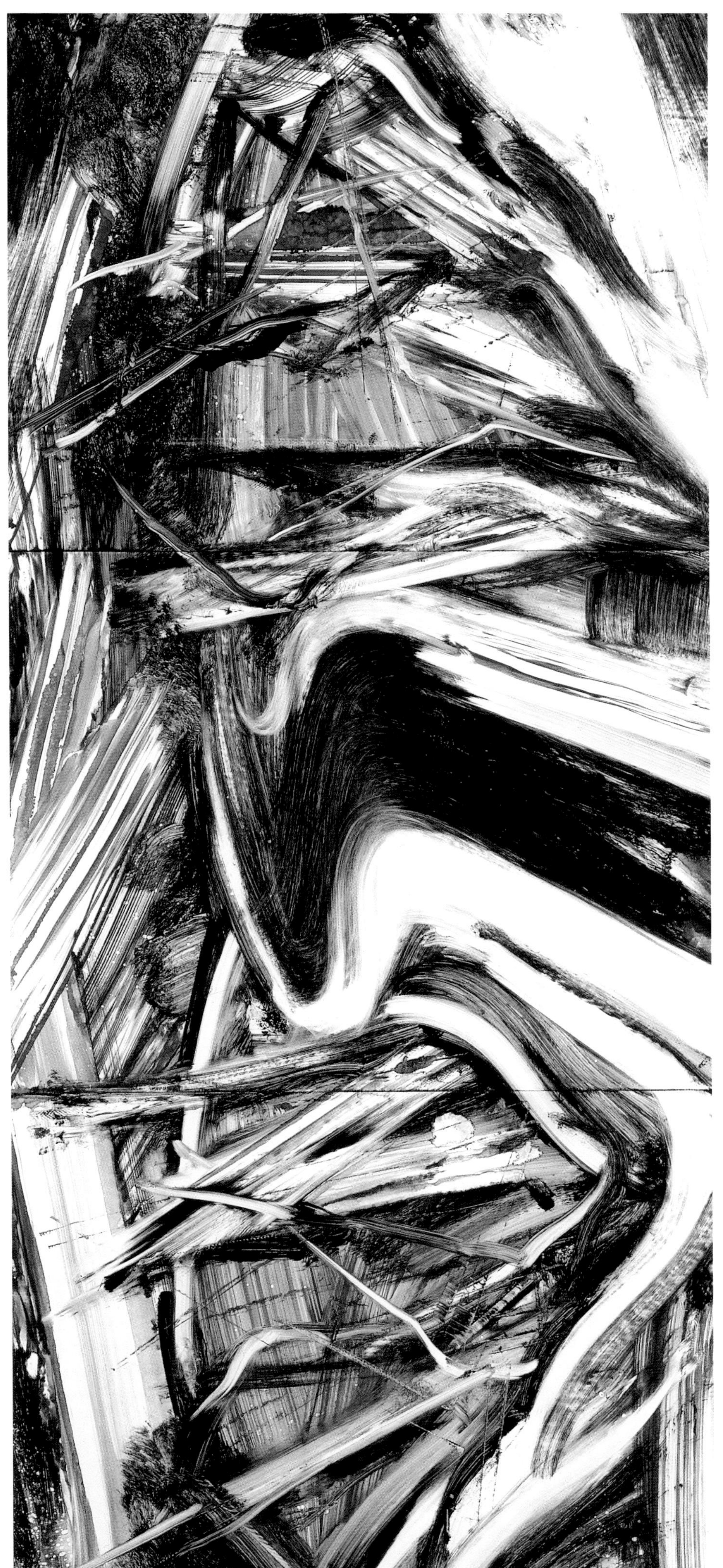

V, 10. 26. 99

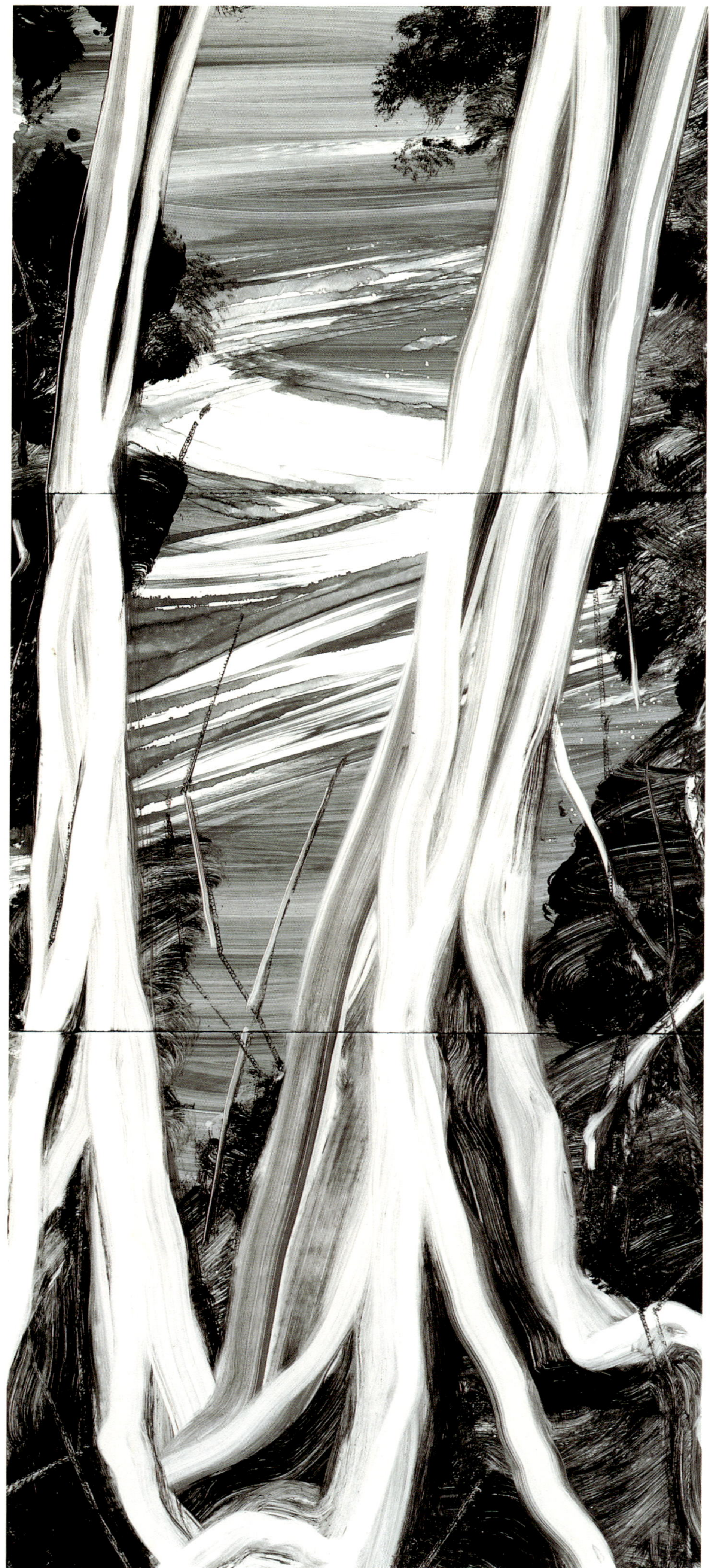

III, 10. 26. 99

All monotypes are **Untitled** and printed on Arches Cover White by Maurice Sanchez
at Derrière L'Etoile Studios, New York in October of 1999.

Monotypes reproduced on first and last pages are 13 x 18 ½ inches, 33 x 47 cm.

Monotypes reproduced in small horizontal format are 25 x 42 inches, 63.5 x 106.7 cm.

Monotypes reproduced in large vertical format are 79 x 38 inches, 200.7 x 97.8 cm.

Monotypes reproduced in large horizontal format are 79 x 38 inches, 200.7 x 97.8 cm.

Monotype: a unique print made without the use of a fixed matrix, usually by painting or drawing on an unmarked metal or glass plate which is then run through the press.

Although the process of printing transfers most of the ink from the plate to the paper, second impressions, called "ghosts" or "cognates", can be printed or used as the ground for further invention by the artist. The proces was invented in the seventeenth century by a Genoese painter and etcher, Giovanni Benedetto Castiglione.

Robert Zandvliet was born in Terband, The Netherlands in 1970. He has had several one-man exhibitions. The first at Witte de With, Rotterdam and Galerie Onrust, Amsterdam, 1995; then in 1996 at the Dordrechts Museum, Dordrecht and in 1997 at De Pont Foundation for Contemporary Art, Tilburg. In 1999 his paintings were exhibited at Galerie naechst St. Stephan, Vienna and most recently at the Musee d'art moderne et contemporain, Strassbourg, France and Peter Blum, New York in spring of 2000. He lives and works in Rotterdam.

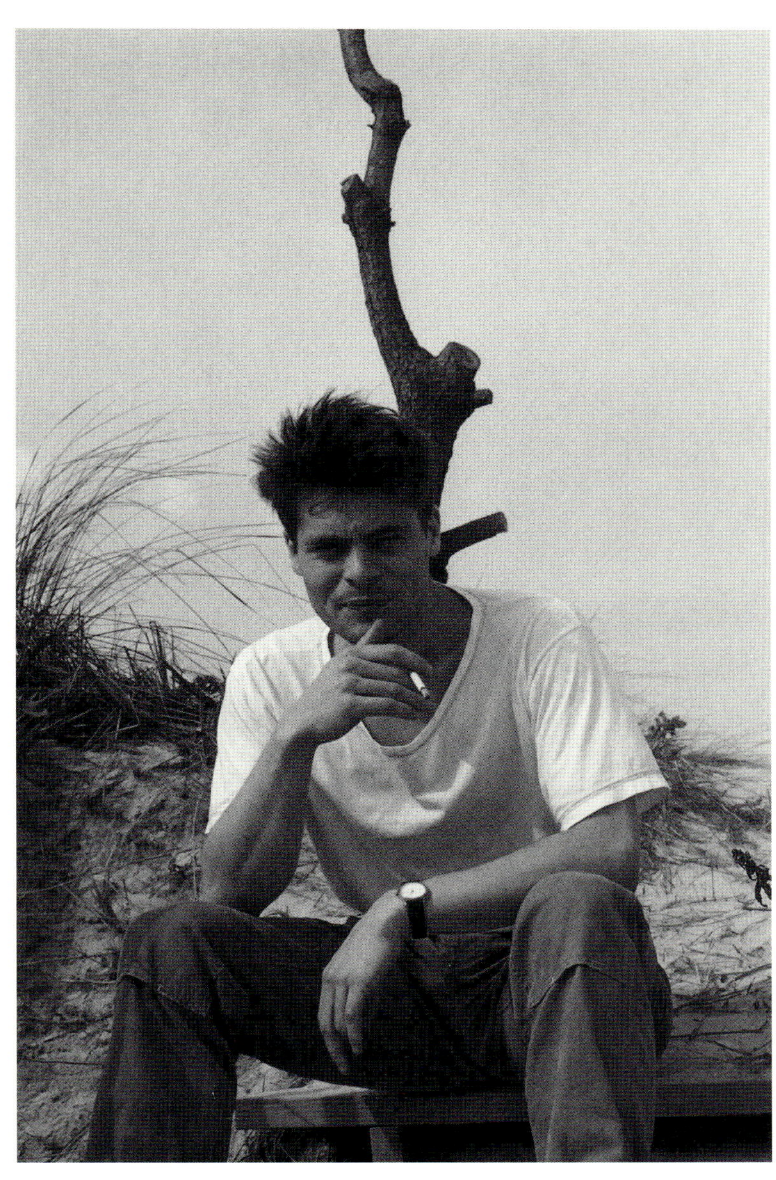

Robert Zandvliet, Bridgehampton, N.Y., October 1999

Vincent Katz was born in 1960 in New York City. He is the author of several books of poetry, including *A Tremor In The Morning*, with linocuts by Alex Katz (Peter Blum Edition, 1986), *Cabal Of Zealots* (Hanuman Books, 1988), *Boulevard Transportation*, with photographs by Rudy Burckhardt (Tibor de Nagy Editions, 1997), and *Pearl*, with paintings by Tabboo! (powerHouse Books, 1998). In 1995, he published *Charm*, translations from Latin of the poet Sextus Propertius (Sun & Moon Press). He is the author of *Life Is Paradise: The Portraits Of Francesco Clemente* (powerHouse Books, 1999). He currently lives in New York City.

Elaine Equi was born in 1953 in Oak Park, Illinois. She is the author of many books including *Surface Tension*, *Decoy* and most recently *Voice-Over*, which won the 1998 San Francisco State Poetry Award. Her work has also been widely anthologized and appears in such places as *The Best American Poetry 1989, The Best American Poetry 1995* and *A Norton Anthology of Postmodern American Poetry.* She lives in New York City.

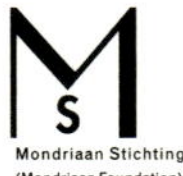

Supported by the Mondriaan Foundation, Amsterdam, The Netherlands

Book design by Jean Robert, Robert & Durrer, Zürich, Switzerland
Photo of Robert Zandvliet by Peter Blum

Lythography by Egli. Kunz & Partner, Glattbrugg ZH, Switzerland
Printed by Waser Druck AG, Buchs ZH, Switzerland
Bookbinding by Buchbinderei Burkardt AG Mönchaltorf ZH, Switzerland

Published by Peter Blum Edition, Blumarts, Inc., New York, 2000
Copyright © by the authors.

ISBN 0-935875-18-2
Printed in Switzerland

This book has been published on the occasion of the exhibition Robert Zandvliet at Peter Blum, New York in the spring of 2000, in an edition of fifteen hundred copies.

There is a special edition of two hundred signed and numbered copies, the first ninety copies are accompanied by an original monotype.

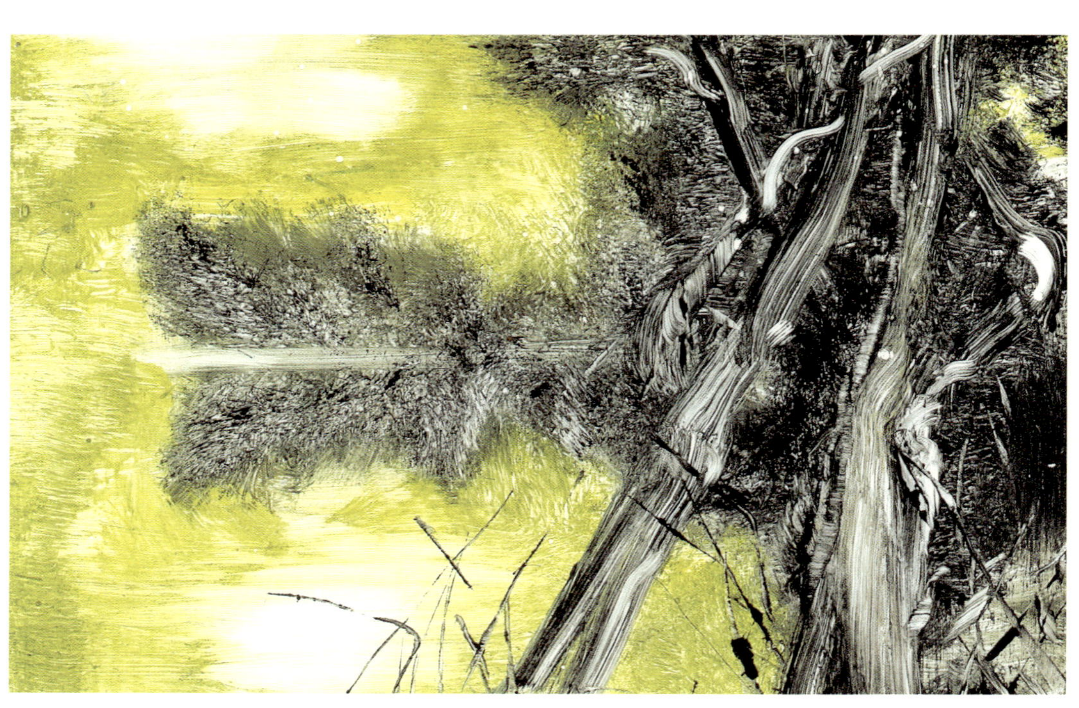